The Blue Badge Guide's

EDINBURGH
Quiz Book

John A. Duncan

The History Press

First published 2017

The History Press
The Mill, Brimscombe Port
Stroud, Gloucestershire, GL5 2QG
www.thehistorypress.co.uk

British Library Cataloguing in Publication Data.

A catalogue record for this book is available from the British Library.

ISBN 978 0 7509 8350 1

Typesetting and origination by The History Press
Printed and bound by CPI Group (UK) Ltd

Contents

Foreword

Having spent part of my education in Edinburgh and many years visiting our historic capital city there are so many parts of it that I have still to discover. It's an amazingly fascinating city with subjects and history that will catch the imagination of many a visitor. Of course, in order to discover our great past the knowledge of a great guide is essential.

Thanks to the painstaking work done by John you can tour the various aspects of Edinburgh and have a little fun with family and friends, just to make sure that they have been paying attention.

This wonderful quiz book will be a great addition to both locals' and visitors' bookshelves, who, I am sure, will by proud to share their new-found knowledge.

Torquhil Campbell
Duke of Argyll
Hon. President Scottish Tourist Guides Association (STGA)

Introduction

Twenty or so years ago I knew an Italian girl, originally from Padua near Venice, who was then working in Edinburgh. One December evening we were walking down the Gardens side of Princes Street when she suddenly stopped, clutched my arm, and, looking at the illuminated Old Town running down the slope from the castle, gasped, 'Oh, this beautiful city!' I have never forgotten that moment; she always maintained that Edinburgh was the most beautiful city in Europe, and, given where she came from, that seems no ordinary compliment!

For Edinburgh is indeed a beautiful city. In large measure this is the gift of nature – the dramatic Old Town ridge; the volcanic hills that surround and form part of the city centre; the long slope down through the New Town to the Firth of Forth. All these conspire to provide Edinburgh with outstanding vistas whichever way you look. The city's very steepness adds excitement and interest at every turn.

This bounty of nature has been enhanced by the quality of the city's architecture, and the farsightedness of its town planning. The crowded medieval layout of the Old Town is perfectly complemented by the spacious streets, circuses and gardens of the Georgian New Town. No wonder they have been awarded the accolade of UNESCO World Heritage status.

But Edinburgh is not merely beautiful: it is endlessly fascinating. Inhabited for well over 2,000 years and the Royal capital of Scotland since the fifteenth century, its history is largely that of the country itself; and it has accumulated over the centuries a bottomless trove of myth, tradition and legend.

How are visitors to make sense of all there is to see and learn? By far their surest bet is to explore the city in the company of a Scottish Blue Badge Guide. In order to gain their Blue Badge these guides have all successfully completed an in-depth two-year training course and passed the rigorous admission examinations of the Scottish Tourist Guides Association (STGA). The STGA Blue Badge qualification is accredited by the World Federation of Tourist Guide Associations, and is mutually recognised by our colleagues in England, Wales and Northern Ireland.

STGA members are the only professionally qualified tourist guides based in Scotland, and our training is not confined to learning facts and data, though of course this is vital. We are also taught the guiding skills we need to give our guests the full package – enjoyable, entertaining and informative. Nearly all our clients are in Scotland on holiday, and we never lose sight of the fact that they are here to have fun. Our Blue Badge members are qualified to guide anywhere in Scotland, so they can take you all over the country, not just Edinburgh.

How do you book a Scottish Blue Badge guide? The best approach is to visit the STGA's website, www.stga.co.uk, where you will find all our members listed with brief information about the services they offer and their contact details. In most cases, though, it is easier to use the STGA's own booking service, either through the online form or by telephoning the contact number +44(0)1786 451 953. Our dedicated booking team will be happy to help you select the ideal guide for the tour you have in mind.

This quiz book attempts to give you something of the flavour of exploring Edinburgh in the company of a Blue Badge guide. So imagine that you are stepping off with a knowledgeable, entertaining companion as I take you on a series of tours looking into different aspects of the city's history, culture and environment.

This book comprises twenty-two themed 'rounds', each containing ten questions. The questions in each round start off relatively simple and become progressively more difficult – by the end you should know rather more about Edinburgh than most natives of the city!

John A. Duncan, 2017
Chairman, Scottish Tourist Guides Association
www.stga.co.uk

About the Author

John Duncan is a native of Glasgow, although he has lived in Edinburgh for over twenty years. Despite the traditional rivalry between the two cities, he now feels equally at home in either!

John's degree from the University of Glasgow is in Classics and Ancient History, but while there he also studied Scottish History. Ever since he has had a passion for the history, culture and landscapes of Scotland which he is now able to share with visitors from around the world as a Scottish Blue Badge guide.

After graduation he trained as a Scottish Chartered Accountant, and his career with a number of international accounting firms took him, among other places, to Hong Kong for five years, followed by a spell in London before he eventually escaped back to Scotland. He has been based in Edinburgh since 1994.

After leaving the accountancy profession for the voluntary sector, he spent seven years as Chief Executive of a major educational charity, where his primary focus was on developing young people's abilities in speaking, debating and effective communication. Finally he felt called to apply his passion for Scotland and his communication skills more directly, and started his training to become a Scottish Blue Badge Guide in 2010.

Since qualifying in spring 2012, John has developed a diverse practice that takes him all over Scotland with groups both large and small. Whilst many of his tours are general in nature, his specialist interests lie in all aspects of Scottish history (including that of religion), Scottish literature – and whisky!

John has served on the Board of the Scottish Tourist Guides Association since 2013 and was elected National Chairman in April 2015, following a spell as Chairman of the STGA's Edinburgh Branch.

Acknowledgements

I owe deep thanks to several people, without whose cheerful assistance this book could not have been written. Firstly to three of my Scottish Blue Badge colleagues, Susan Shedden, Alison Reid and Sally Duncanson, who made many helpful suggestions as I was writing it and proofread the final draft for howlers. Secondly to two non-guiding friends, Colin Eckford and Brian Gorman, who cast a 'layman's' eye over both questions and answers. Next to Mark King, the writer of the companion *The Blue Badge Guide's London Quiz Book*, who was a generous source of encouragement and advice. And finally to Matilda Richards at The History Press for initiating this project and steering it safely home.

Old Town

The ancient medieval core of the city, stretching down the ridge from the castle to the Palace of Holyroodhouse, is still Edinburgh's most conspicuous landmark. Some 60,000 people lived within this confined space by the 1760s. In this first round we wander down some of the Old Town's nooks and crannies.

1. What is the Royal Mile, and why is it so called?

2. What is a forestair?

3. What is the oldest house in Edinburgh?

4. What is the Mercat Cross?

5. True or false: the street name 'Canongate' comes from a former Royal artillery park at Holyrood Palace at the foot of the Royal Mile.

6. What was the name of the main gate in the City Wall at the foot of High Street?

7. What would have been your reaction in Old Edinburgh if someone overhead cried out 'Gardyloo!'?

8. What were the Luckenbooths?

9. What was the original function of the City Chambers?

10. What was a caddie?

Enough of the 'Old', now let's look at the 'New'.

Answers - Round 1

1. The long main street of the Old Town, running
    down the crag and tail ridge from the castle
    to the Queen's Palace of Holyroodhouse

It is so called because it connects a royal castle with a royal palace, and is just over a mile long. It actually consists of five streets that connect end to end. Starting at the Castle Esplanade, we go down Castlehill, followed by Lawnmarket, High Street, Canongate and finally Abbey Strand which leads to the gates of the palace. The name Royal Mile itself is of comparatively recent origin, being first coined in a guidebook published in 1901.

2. An external open stair leading to
    the first floor of a building

Typical of old Edinburgh, the ground floor of buildings facing on to the street was used for shops and other commercial premises. The forestair gave direct access to the residential apartments above. Most of the Old Town's forestairs were swept away long ago, as they were already considered an obstruction to pedestrians, but there are some picturesque survivals – for example at Gladstone's Land in the Lawnmarket and Moubray House on High Street.

3. John Knox House on High Street

However, the adjacent Moubray House may well vie for the honour of being Edinburgh's oldest house, as both have elements believed to date back to the closing decades of the fifteenth century. Both were extensively rebuilt after the burning of Edinburgh by the Earl of Hertford's English army in 1544, and the present frontage of John Knox House is mid-sixteenth century, while that of Moubray House is early seventeenth. Despite its traditional association with John Knox, it is now thought unlikely that the fiery reformer actually lived in the house that bears his name, although he would have known it when he was minister of St Giles further up the Royal Mile in the 1560s and '70s. Daniel Defoe, the author of *Robinson Crusoe*, lived in Moubray House in 1706-7, when he was an English spy working for the passage of the Act of Union.

4. The sign of Edinburgh's status as a burgh, with the right to hold a market, to raise local taxes and to be self-governing

Burgh status was awarded by charter from the king (royal burgh), the Church (ecclesiastical burgh), or the local lord (burgh of barony). Typically, a mercat cross takes the form of a pillar crowned by a heraldic carving. Edinburgh's cross is now situated at the eastern end of St Giles, opposite the City Chambers, though this is not its original location, which is marked in the paving slabs slightly further down High Street, in front of the statue of Adam Smith. The present cross was erected in 1885 at the expense of W.E. Gladstone, the famous Victorian statesman who was a local MP. It takes the form of an octagonal drum-shaped base with heraldic arms on each face, while the shaft of the cross, topped by a unicorn, rises from the base. The platform on top of the base is the place in Scotland where Royal Proclamations are read by the Lord Lyon King of Arms.

5. False

The name derives from the canons, or clergy, of Holyrood Abbey. Literally it means 'The Canons' Street', and the name was also applied to the ecclesiastical burgh founded at the same time as the Abbey in the 1120s. Canongate remained a separate burgh until 1856, when it was finally absorbed within the City of Edinburgh.

6. The Netherbow Port

This was an imposing castellated and turreted structure, erected in its latter form when the city walls were recon- structed after Scotland's disastrous defeat by the English at Flodden in 1513. Despite its formidable appearance, Bonnie Prince Charlie's Jacobite army captured it by a ruse in September 1745, sneaking through the gates when they were opened to admit a delegation of magistrates who had been negotiating with the Jacobite force. As a result, Edinburgh (but not the castle) was captured without a single shot being fired. The Netherbow Port was demolished in 1764 as an obstruction to traffic, but its outline is marked by brass plates on the road surface at the junction of High Street and the Canongate. A carved wall-mounted plaque on the north side of High Street, just above the junction, gives a good impression of how it once looked.

7. Move quickly out of the way!

Old Edinburgh had to build high in order to squeeze so many people into such a compact area. Many 'lands' on the Royal Mile rose to eight storeys or more, while, because of the steepness of the slope, they were even higher down the narrow closes and wynds descending on either side to the 'Nor' Loch' (where Princes Street Gardens are now) and to the Cowgate. There was no running water in those days, and so no flushing lavatories. Each evening, at the beat of a drum, people threw from their windows whatever unpleasantness had accumulated during the day, to the shout of 'Gardy-loo!' (from the French *Prenez garde à l'eau* – 'watch out for the water'). If you were passing underneath when this cry rang out you would exclaim – perhaps more in hope than expectation – 'Haud yer haun' ('Hold your hand'). I fear, though, that history records that all too often people were the victims of these rather unsavoury showers!

8. The Luckenbooths were a long narrow row of tenements that used to stand in the centre of High Street, immediately north of St Giles

Dating originally from the mid-fifteenth century, but frequently rebuilt and extended, they housed lockable shops (the meaning of the word). The eastern end of the Luckenbooths, facing down High Street, was where the poet Alan Ramsay opened a bookshop and Edinburgh's first circulating library in the eighteenth century. This was later taken over by William Creech, the publisher of Robert Burns, who regularly frequented the shop along with most of the city's literati. The narrow passage between this building and St Giles was known as 'the Krames', and was filled with the open stalls of toy sellers. The Luckenbooths were demolished in 1817, to open up the street. Their former outline is marked by brass plates in the roadway.

9. The original function of the City Chambers was as the Royal Exchange for the use of the city's merchants

It was officially opened in 1760 by George Drummond, the pioneering Lord Provost who was also the driving force behind the creation of the New Town. Edinburgh's merchants had traditionally done their trading in the open air by the Mercat Cross (in its previous location – see 4 above). This had been taken down in 1756, largely to encourage merchants to use the new facility, but they continued to prefer dealing at the Cross's former site or in the many taverns in the area. As a result, the City Council took over much of the building in 1811, and by the end of the nineteenth century occupied it all. It was designed by John Adam, the son of William and brother of the more famous Robert.

10. In old Edinburgh, a caddie (or cadie) was a ubiquitous necessity, a curious combination of messenger, delivery man, news vendor and guide

The Old Town was full of dark closes and narrow, badly lit stairs. There were no street names or house numbers, so often the only way to find your way to a particular apartment or have a message delivered was to engage the services of a caddie, who knew all the city's nooks and crannies, where everyone lived, and everyone's business. From the beginning of the eighteenth century they were licenced and regulated by the City Council – rather like taxi drivers today – and became a closed company, subject to rules and discipline. Many of them were Highlanders. They disappeared in the early nineteenth century, after the successful development of the New Town. As a matter of interest, the golfing term 'caddy' probably comes from the fact that Edinburgh gentlemen hired caddies to carry their clubs when they were playing a round of golf.

ROUND 2

New Town

Let's leave the crowded huddle of the Old Town and head across to the Georgian elegance of the New Town. Conceived from the outset as a planned development, its spacious, gracious streets and squares soon became the home of Edinburgh's more prosperous citizens. Construction of the original New Town started in 1767 and was largely complete by 1800, although further extensions continued to be built to the north and west up to the second half of the nineteenth century. How at home are you in the New Town?

1. Who won the competition for the design of the first New Town?

2. After whom is Princes Street named?

3. Where is Bute House, and who lives there?

4. Where did most of the building stone for the New Town come from?

5. Whose statue tops the column in St Andrew Square?

6. Which building has a lighthouse above its doorway, and why?

7. Which major national organisation is based at 121 George Street?

8. How did Picardy Place get its name?

9. Which world-famous inventor was born at 14 South Charlotte Street in 1847?

10. How did St David Street acquire its name?

Now we've had an initial look at both Old and New Towns, time to go into some more detail.

Answers - Round 2

1. James Craig (1739-1795)

For years George Drummond, Lord Provost until 1764, had been the driving force behind the idea of building a 'new town' on the other side of the glacial valley from the Old Town. Already by 1765 a start had been made on draining the Nor' Loch (where Princes Street gardens now are) and on Constructing North Bridge, the first link across the valley. In January 1766, a competition was held to design the layout of the New Town, and Craig's winning entry made clever use of the natural lie of the land. A main axial street on the top of the ridge (George Street) linked two grand squares at either end, while additional main streets were planned to the north (Queen Street) and the south (Princes Street). These were formed into a grid by linking cross streets, while narrower service streets lay between the three main thoroughfares. Craig did not design the buildings, merely the shape of the town. Construction was undertaken by various developers building individual plots, starting at the east end in 1767 and culminating in the west with Charlotte Square, which was completed in the early nineteenth century.

2. The sons of King George III

Note that it is Princes (plural) and not Prince's (singular). Nearly all the streets of the original new town were given names either honouring the Royal Family or celebrating the Union between Scotland and England. Thus we have George Street after the king, while both Queen Street and Charlotte Square are named after Queen Charlotte. Rose

Street is matched by Thistle Street, while St Andrew Square was originally to be matched by St George's Square. This last was renamed Charlotte Square to avoid confusion with George Square on the south side of the city. These names declare Edinburgh's loyalty to the House of Hanover in the aftermath of the Jacobite risings earlier in the century.

3. Number 6 Charlotte Square; and the
First Minister of Scotland

Bute House is in the centre of the north façade of Robert Adam's classical masterpiece which is generally considered one of the finest urban squares in Europe. Sadly, Adam did not live to see his design completed, dying in 1792. The house is named after the 4th Marquess of Bute, who bought numbers 5, 6 and 7 in the early twentieth century. In 1966, after the death of the 5th Marquess, it was accepted by the Treasury in lieu of death duties, and conveyed to the National Trust for Scotland, who still own it. From 1970 until devolution in 1999 it was the official residence of the Secretary of State for Scotland. Since then it has been the official residence of the First Minister.

4. Craigleith Quarry, about two miles
north-west of the New Town

The quarry produced extremely high-grade blonde sandstone, but was virtually worked out by the end of the nineteenth century, although some minor quarrying went on until the Second World War. It was completely infilled by the early 1990s, and is now the site of a Sainsbury's superstore and retail park.

5. Henry Dundas, 1st Viscount Melville (1742–1811)

Dundas was an astute Tory statesman and consummate political fixer, who virtually controlled Scottish politics for Pitt the Younger at the end of the eighteenth and start of the nineteenth centuries – so much so that he was nicknamed 'King Harry the 9th'. The monument comprises a 136-foot column topped by a 14-foot statue of Dundas, giving a total height of 150 feet. It was erected in 1823, to the design of the architect William Burn. The statue was carved by Robert Forrest.

6. 84 George Street, the headquarters of the Northern Lighthouse Board, which is in charge of all lighthouses in Scottish waters

Many of Scotland's most iconic lighthouses were designed by the Stevenson family, into which the writer Robert Louis Stevenson was born in 1850. All Scottish lighthouses have been automated since 1998, but there is still a control room at 84 George Street from which they are supervised and managed. As far as we are aware, there have been no shipwrecks on George Street since the lighthouse was installed!

7. The Church of Scotland, Scotland's national church, has its headquarters here

Presbyterian in its governance and Reformed in its theology, the Kirk (as it is generally known) has been a pervasive influence on Scottish society and culture since the Protestant Reformation in 1560. With around 1,500 parishes across Scotland, the Kirk covers every square mile of the country.

8. Picardy Place originates from the area of that name in France

In the early eighteenth century a small group of migrant silk workers from France were settled, at the city's invitation, to the north-west of Calton Hill. As they were Huguenots from the Picardie region, the area where they set up home became known as 'Picardy Village'. When the New Town extended eastwards to absorb this area around 1809-10, the name was transferred to the new street, which became Picardy Place.

9. Alexander Graham Bell, the inventor of the telephone

This is commemorated by a plaque on the building. Curiously, South Charlotte Street, linking Charlotte Square and Princes Street, is only about 100 yards long, and on both corners to Princes Street are mobile phone shops. Thus we have the entire history of telecommunications summed up in one short Edinburgh street!

10. After David Hume, the famous philosopher

He was one of the earliest residents of the street – then unnamed – and was notorious for his scepticism if not out-right atheism. A waggish minister ironically chalked on the wall of his dwelling 'Saint David's Street' – and so it has remained to the present day!

ROUND 3

Royal Edinburgh

As the ancient seat of Scotland's kings and still the home of a working Royal Palace, Edinburgh has associations with royalty that are long and deep. In this round we'll humbly explore this regal past and present.

1. What are the Honours of Scotland, and where may they be found?

2. Where may you see the former Royal Yacht *Britannia*?

3. Where in Edinburgh did Bonnie Prince Charlie stay in 1745?

4. Who form the Queen's official bodyguard in Scotland?

5. What is the Thistle Ceremony, and where does it take place?

6. What lines the walls of the Great Gallery in the Palace of Holyroodhouse?

7. Who was murdered in Holyrood Palace in 1566?

8. Who stays at Holyrood Palace every May?

9. Which future King of England was born in Edinburgh Castle?

10. What infamous dinner took place in Edinburgh Castle in November 1440?

Now that we've met royalty, it's time to get religious.

Answers - Round 3

1. The Honours of Scotland are the Scottish
   Crown Jewels, comprising Crown, Sceptre
   and Sword of State, in Edinburgh Castle

These date back to the fifteenth and sixteenth centuries, and are the oldest regalia in Britain. Unlike the English Crown Jewels, which were melted down under Oliver Cromwell and had to be made anew after the Restoration, their Scottish counterparts were successfully hidden from Cromwell's troops in Aberdeenshire. Until the Act of Union in 1707, the Honours were displayed at each sitting of the old Scottish Parliament, and royal assent to legislation was indicated by touching the Act with the Sceptre. After the Union they were locked in a chest and taken to Edinburgh Castle and forgotten until, in 1818, Sir Walter Scott rediscovered them. Since then they have been on public display and may be seen in the Crown Room in the castle.

2. At Ocean Terminal in Leith

The Royal Yacht *Britannia* was built on the Clyde in 1953, and until 1997 sailed the world on the Queen's official visits, as well as providing a holiday retreat for Her Majesty and members of the Royal Family. Following her decommissioning (without replacement) in 1997, she was acquired in April 1998 by The Royal Yacht Britannia Trust, a Scottish-registered charity, and since then has been at Leith as a major world-class visitor attraction.

3. At the Palace of Holyroodhouse

After the Jacobites bloodlessly captured Edinburgh (but not the castle) in September 1745, Prince Charles Edward Stuart held court at Holyrood for five weeks until he led his army south into England. The rising ended unhappily at the Battle of Culloden in April 1746, when the Jacobites were routed by a Government army under the Duke of Cumberland, George II's youngest son. The savage repression of the Highland clans in the rebellion's aftermath earned the Duke the soubriquet of 'Butcher Cumberland'.

4. The Royal Company of Archers

Originally formed in 1676, it obtained a Royal Charter in 1713 and has been the monarch's official bodyguard in Scotland since 1822. Numbering around 400 active members, all of whom have to be of Scottish blood, it has traditionally been the preserve of the 'great and good' of Scottish society, including many members of the nobility. The Company has its own Edinburgh base in Archers' Hall in Buccleuch Street, and continues to practise with its traditional weapons, holding a number of annual archery competitions.

5. The annual service of the Order of the Thistle, Scotland's most senior order of chivalry. It takes place in the Thistle Chapel in the High Kirk of St Giles

The Order was founded by James VII in 1687, and is limited to sixteen knights, excluding members of the Royal Family. The Thistle Chapel was designed by the renowned Scottish architect Sir Robert Lorimer, and completed in 1911. Ornate carved wooden stalls line the chapel, each one surmounted by the heraldic helm of its incumbent knight.

6. The portraits of 110 kings of Scotland, from the
   legendary Fergus I to Charles II, who commissioned them

They were all painted by the Dutch artist Jacob de Wet
between 1684 and 1686. For nearly all these monarchs, of
course, de Wet had to rely on his imagination rather than
any genuine likeness. Perhaps this is why most of them
seem to display a striking resemblance to Charles II, especially around the nose!

7. David Rizzio

An Italian courtier of Mary Queen of Scots, originally
employed as a musician, Rizzio had risen to become the
Queen's secretary, confidant and friend. In doing so he
aroused the jealous suspicions of Mary's husband, Henry
Lord Darnley. Several powerful Scottish nobles also resented
Rizzio's influence with the Queen and easily fanned Darnley's
smouldering jealousy into flames. On 9 March 1566, Mary
was dining with Rizzio and the Countess of Argyll in a small
closet just off her bedchamber. When Darnley and some of
the other conspirators appeared in the room it was clear that
mischief was afoot. Rizzio attempted to shelter behind the
Queen (who was heavily pregnant), but rough hands dragged
him into an adjacent chamber where he was stabbed fifty-
six times. The rooms where this appalling crime took place
can still be visited in the Palace of Holyroodhouse.

8. The Lord High Commissioner to the General
   Assembly of the Church of Scotland

Unlike with the Church of England, of which she is by law
the Supreme Governor, the Queen is merely a member of the
Church of Scotland, which recognises no other Head than the

Lord Jesus Christ. However, the position of the Kirk as the National Church is enshrined in statute, and every May, when its General Assembly is held on the Mound, the Sovereign is represented by the Lord High Commissioner. When the Assembly is in session, the Lord High Commissioner resides at the Palace, and ranks third in the Scottish Order of Precedence, after the Sovereign and the Duke of Edinburgh.

9. James I (and VI of Scotland)

After Rizzio's murder (see 7 above), Mary skilfully detached Darnley from the other conspirators and determined that, for security, she would give birth to her expected child behind the strong ramparts of Edinburgh Castle. Here, on 19 June 1566, was born the little prince who, a year later, on the forced abdication of his mother, would be proclaimed King James VI. After the death of the childless Elizabeth I of England in 1603 he, as nearest heir, also became James I of England in what is known as the Union of the Crowns. So remember, when talking of the Union of Scotland and England, that Scotland took England over, and not the other way round!

10. The Black Dinner

In 1440 King James II was a boy of 10, and controlled by his unscrupulous guardians, Sir William Crichton and Sir Alexander Livingstone. They feared and resented the power of the great Douglas family, and invited the 6th Earl of Douglas, a lad of 16, and his younger brother to dine with the boy king in Edinburgh Castle. While they ate in the Great Hall a black bull's head, the symbol of death, was carried in and placed before the Earl. The two Douglases were immediately dragged out of the Hall, given a mock trial and executed by beheading.

ROUND 4

Religious Edinburgh

Since the Protestant Reformation in the sixteenth century, Edinburgh has been the focus of the religious life of the nation, but there has been Christian worship in the city since at least the seventh century. Maybe you should offer a brief prayer that you know the answers to the following questions!

1. Where does the General Assembly of the Church of Scotland take place each May?

2. Which Scottish king founded Holyrood Abbey?

3. Where does HM the Queen worship when in residence at Holyrood Palace?

4. Why is St Giles Cathedral arguably a misnomer?

5. To which denomination does St Mary's Cathedral on Palmerston Place belong?

6. What is the oldest religious building in Edinburgh to survive intact?

7. Who was the principal leader of the Reformation in Scotland?

8. Which is the only church in Edinburgh to hold regular Sunday services in Gaelic?

9. What major event, affecting churches and congregations across Scotland, took place at St Andrew's and St George's West Church in George Street in May 1843?

10. How is 'The Mosque of the Custodian of the Two Holy Mosques' better known?

*You can get off your knees now –
it's time to read a good book!*

Answers – Round 4

1. The General Assembly Hall on top of the Mound

This was originally built in the 1840s for the Free Church of Scotland, but after most of the Free Church re-joined the Church of Scotland in 1929 it became the Assembly Hall for the newly united Church. Previously the Church of Scotland had held its General Assembly in the old Tolbooth Church (now The Hub, the Edinburgh Festival Centre), whose towering spire still overshadows the General Assembly Hall.

2. King David I, in 1128

The traditional story of its foundation is that King David was hunting in the park at the foot of the Salisbury Crags when he was thrown from his horse by a monstrous stag that threatened to gore him with its antlers. At this, a vision of the Holy Cross appeared between the antlers of the stag, which immediately took flight. In thanks for his miraculous deliverance, the king vowed to establish an abbey on the site. Whatever the truth of the tale, King David certainly founded an Augustinian abbey there – one of the many religious foundations which that pious king established across Scotland. Note that 'rood' is an old word for cross, so the name Holyrood means 'Holy Cross'.

3. The Canongate Kirk

Construction of this church was ordered at the end of the seventeenth century by James VII, who wished to make Holyrood Abbey (until then used as the parish church for the Canongate) into a splendid chapel for his new Order of the

Thistle. He never saw it completed however, as in 1688 he was forced from the thrones of Scotland and England in the 'Glorious Revolution'.

4. Because it is not a cathedral!

A cathedral is a church holding the 'cathedra' or throne of a bishop, and the Presbyterian Church of Scotland does not have any bishops. Even before the Protestant Reformation of 1560 it was not a cathedral but a collegiate church, as Edinburgh was part of the diocese of St Andrews. There were two brief periods during the seventeenth century (1635–38 and 1660–89) when St Giles *was* a cathedral, as first Charles I and then his son Charles II attempted to impose episcopacy on the reluctant Scots. It is more properly referred to as the High Kirk of St Giles, but everyone knows it as St Giles Cathedral.

5. The Scottish Episcopal Church

Although part of the Anglican Communion, this church has no historical connection with the Church of England. Rather it descends from those in the Church of Scotland who, for reasons of conscience, were unwilling to accept the Presbyterian settlement of 1690. In the first half of the eighteenth century many Scottish Episcopalians were supporters of the Jacobite cause. St Mary's Cathedral itself dominates the western skyline of central Edinburgh with its three massive spires. Construction of this vast edifice started in 1874, although the twin spires on the western towers were not completed until 1917. These two spires are named 'Barbara' and 'Mary', after the Walker sisters whose generosity had funded the Cathedral's construction.

6. St Margaret's Chapel in Edinburgh Castle

Dating from around 1130, this is not only the oldest church but the oldest building in Edinburgh, and is still used for weddings. It was built by David I in memory of his mother, Queen Margaret, who had died in the castle in 1093. Renowned for her piety, this Saxon Princess had married King Malcolm III around 1070. She was canonised in 1250, Scotland's only royal saint – so far.

7. John Knox (1513-1572)

Born in East Lothian, he was ordained a Catholic priest but soon came under the influence of early Scottish reformers such as George Wishart, and of the intellectual and religious ferment that had been unleashed on the Continent in the aftermath of Martin Luther's 'Ninety-five Theses' of 1517. After an adventurous career that took him to England, Frankfurt and Geneva (where he became an admirer of John Calvin), he returned to Scotland in 1559, where his fiery and inspiring leadership was pivotal in ensuring the success of the Protestant Reformation in 1560. At this crucial time he became the Minister of St Giles, a position he retained until his death in 1572. Mary Queen of Scots returned to Scotland in 1561, still a devout Roman Catholic, and Knox had a number of memorable confrontations with her in which he refused to bend or compromise, and on one occasion reducing her to tears.

8. Greyfriars Kirk

A Gaelic service is held here each Sunday at 12.30 p.m., carrying on a continuous tradition started in Edinburgh in 1704 at a variety of churches around the city. Latterly the

Gaelic services were held in the Highland Tolbooth Church (now The Hub), but when that congregation merged with Greyfriars in 1979 the services moved with them.

9. The Great Disruption

Despite the Church of Scotland's right to exercise independent jurisdiction over its spiritual affairs being recognised in the Treaty of Union of 1707, the Westminster Parliament soon moved to limit that independence. In particular, it imposed on the Kirk the 'right of patronage' – that is the right of a wealthy patron to install a minister of his choice in a parish regardless of the views of the congregation and the kirk session. This proved a long-festering sore that many in the Kirk, particularly Evangelicals, bitterly resented, and culminated in a number of legal cases in the 1830s which the Evangelical party lost. Finally, in May 1843, at the General Assembly held in what was then St Andrew's Church in George Street, 121 ministers and seventy-three elders walked out of the Assembly to form the Free Church of Scotland – an event known as the Great Disruption. Eventually almost 500 out of some 1,200 ministers joined the breakaway, forfeiting their stipends and manses in the process. Most of the Free Church re-joined the Kirk in 1929, after the principles on which they stood were conceded by Parliament.

10. Edinburgh Central Mosque

The mosque opened in 1998, and serves not just as a place of worship but as a cultural centre for Edinburgh's Muslim population.

ROUND 5

Literary Edinburgh

Edinburgh has a long association with great writers, dating back to at least the late fifteenth century, recognised when it was declared UNESCO's first World City of Literature in 2004. Let's explore that rich heritage and meet some of the literary giants who have lived and worked here over the centuries.

1. True or false: the Scott Monument on Princes Street is the largest monument to a writer built anywhere in the world.

2. In which café on George IV Bridge did J.K. Rowling write much of the first Harry Potter book, *Harry Potter and the Philosopher's Stone*?

3. Three famous Scottish writers are celebrated in The Writers' Museum. Can you name them?

4. Which fictional detective's statue is found in Picardy Place, and why is it there?

5. Which fictional detective drinks in the Oxford Bar in Young Street?

6. Which New Town street is the setting for a series of books by Alexander McCall Smith?

7. Which popular Royal Mile pub has associations with Jekyll and Hyde?

8. Which infamous riot is vividly portrayed in the opening chapters of Sir Walter Scott's *The Heart of Midlothian*?

9. On the fringes of Edinburgh, but now within the city limits, is the picturesque old town of South Queensferry. Which inn there features in both *Kidnapped* by R.L. Stevenson and *The Antiquary* by Sir Walter Scott?

10. What is a 'makar'?

You're pretty well-read now, but next you'll have to do some deep thinking!

Answers – Round 5

1. True
At just over 200 feet high, this towering Gothic pinnacle – aptly described as 'a space rocket designed by monks' – commemorates Sir Walter Scott (1771-1832). After the great man's death, a competition to design a suitable memorial was won by George Meikle Kemp, who sadly did not live to see the monument completed in 1846 – he died in a drowning accident on the Union Canal in 1844. Strongly influenced by the Border abbeys – especially Melrose – Kemp's masterpiece is covered with sixty-four statues, mainly characters from Scott's works. Scott himself is one of the most influential Scotsmen of all time. Not only did the 'Wizard of the North' invent the genre of historical fiction, he can largely be credited with creating the popular image of Scotland worldwide. The publication of his narrative poem *The Lady of the Lake* in 1810 brought huge numbers of visitors north to see for themselves the scenes he had depicted so vividly with his pen, so he may also be responsible for the birth of the Scottish tourism industry!

2. The Elephant House
J.K. Rowling wrote much of *Harry Potter and the Philosopher's Stone*, the first book in the Harry Potter series, in the rear room of this café with its views towards the castle.

3. Sir Walter Scott, Robert Burns and
    Robert Louis Stevenson
Scott's importance to the development of world literature and Scottish culture has already been mentioned, but it is

Robert Burns (1759–1796) that Scots have taken to their heart as the National Bard. Although from Ayrshire in the south west of Scotland, Burns was lionised by Edinburgh society after the first publication of his poems, and spent much time in the city, especially between 1786 and 1787. No other writer in history has more monuments raised in their memory, not just at home but around the globe; while of all writers only Burns has his birth commemorated by annual dinners (known as 'Burns Suppers'). His poetry contains biting satire, uproarious comedy and expressions of the brotherhood of man; while his songs include some of the most tender love lyrics ever penned, as well as perhaps the world's best known song 'Auld Lang Syne'. Edinburgh born and bred, Stevenson spent much of his short life overseas, largely because of his poor health, but never forgot his native land or city – 'When I forget thee, Auld Reekie, may my right hand forget its cunning!' Works such as *Kidnapped*, *Treasure Island* and *The Strange Case of Dr Jekyll and Mr Hyde* will continue to delight and thrill future generations as they have those of the past.

4. Sherlock Holmes

Sir Arthur Conan Doyle, the creator of Sherlock Holmes, was born here in Picardy Place, and this has been celebrated since 1991 by this statue by Gerald Laing. Conan Doyle studied medicine at Edinburgh University, where one of his professors, Joseph Bell, had extraordinary powers of observation and deduction. It was Bell's uncanny abilities that gave Conan Doyle the inspiration for the creation of the world's most famous fictional detective.

5. Inspector John Rebus

Ian Rankin's hard-bitten Edinburgh detective has figured in some twenty books since his first appearance in *Knots and Crosses* in 1987. The Oxford Bar is a tiny, old-fashioned pub in Young Street between George Street and Queen Street, and the hard-drinking Rebus's favourite 'howff'.

6. Scotland Street – number 44, to be precise

Alexander McCall Smith's charming, gentle Scotland Street stories started life as daily episodes in the *Scotsman* newspaper in 2004, appearing in book form later that year with great success. Since then, McCall Smith has continued writing the stories in episodic form in the *Scotsman* for several months each year, making it the longest running serial novel in the world. At the time of writing, eleven volumes have appeared in the series.

7. Deacon Brodie's Tavern

The pub is named after Deacon William Brodie. In the 1780s he was a prosperous cabinet maker and locksmith, a Deacon Convener of Trade and a Town Councillor, but by night he led a gang of thieves. His double life came to an end when he led an unsuccessful armed raid on Edinburgh's Excise Office. Given up by one of his accomplices he fled to the Netherlands, but was arrested there and extradited back to Edinburgh, where he was hanged. Robert Louis Stevenson was fascinated by the split existence of this man – by day a respectable businessman and Town Councillor, by night a Napoleon of crime, and so Brodie achieved an unplanned immortality as the main inspiration for both Dr Jekyll and Mr Hyde.

8. The Porteous Riots

In April 1736 smuggler Andrew Wilson was publicly hanged in the Grassmarket, a few days after his accomplice, George Robertson, had managed to escape. The crowd's sympathies lay with the smuggler, and a riot broke out. The commander of the Town Guard, Captain John Porteous, ordered his men to fire on the mob, resulting in the death of six people. Porteous was charged with murder, convicted, and sentenced to be hanged. Fears arose that he would be reprieved, so on 7 September 1736 a mob several thousand strong stormed the Tolbooth prison where he was being held and dragged the unfortunate officer down the Bow to the Grassmarket, where he was lynched. Sir Walter Scott sets the scene for *Heart of Midlothian* with a vivid depiction of the events of that night.

9. The Hawes Inn

In chapter 6 of *Kidnapped*, young David Balfour is kidnapped from the historic Hawes Inn, while it is also there that, in chapter 2 of *The Antiquary*, William Lovel and Jonathan Oldbuck become better acquainted. The inn is today sheltered under the approach viaduct of the Forth Bridge.

10. A poet or bard

The word is particularly applied to Scots poets of the fifteenth and sixteenth centuries, such as William Dunbar and Robert Henryson. In the twenty-first century the term has been revived to describe publicly funded official poets, first in Edinburgh then in several other Scottish cities. In 2004 the Scottish Parliament established the post of *The Scots Makar* as a national poet laureate for Scotland. Previous holders of the post are Edwin Morgan and Liz Lochhead, while the current Makar is Jackie Kay.

ROUND 6

Enlightenment Edinburgh

In the eighteenth and early nineteenth centuries, Scotland – and especially Edinburgh – became a hub of European culture, with a flood of literary, philosophical and scientific discovery and achievement. It is no coincidence that this era saw the construction of the New Town, with its rational layout and planned elegance. Here we get to know some of the towering figures of that extraordinary time.

1. Which thinker is best known today as the writer of *The Wealth of Nations*?

2. Which Edinburgh-born literary figure is today remembered chiefly as the biographer of Samuel Johnson?

3. Which great French thinker wrote 'We look to Scotland for all our ideas of civilisation'?

4. Which hugely influential philosopher was also a keen amateur cook?

5. In what environs did the great minds of the Edinburgh Enlightenment often debate and socialise?

6. The tombstone of which eighteenth-century poet was paid for by Robert Burns?

7. Who is generally considered the first modern geologist, challenging existing ideas about the age of the earth?

8. Which brilliant professor at Edinburgh University discovered carbon dioxide and latent heat?

9. Which distinguished clergyman and historian was Principal of Edinburgh University for over thirty years in the second half of the eighteenth century?

10. Which eccentric judge and scholar once said that all humans were born with tails, which midwives removed at birth?

That's enough philosophy for now – time for some real fighting!

Answers - Round 6

1. Adam Smith (1723-1790)

Born in Kirkcaldy in Fife, Smith studied at Glasgow and Oxford Universities. In 1751 he started teaching at Glasgow University, and two years later became Professor of Moral Philosophy there. In 1759 he published *The Theory of Moral Sentiments*, and in 1763 became the tutor of the young Duke of Buccleuch, with whom he spent much of the next three years touring Europe. Returning to Kirkcaldy, he devoted most of the next ten years to writing *The Wealth of Nations*. This seminal work, written in elegant Augustan prose, is justly considered the foundation of the modern science of economics. In 1778 he accepted the post of Commissioner of Customs for Scotland, and moved to Edinburgh, where he was close friends with many key figures of the Enlightenment. He is buried in the Canongate Kirkyard, just a few yards up the Royal Mile from his home at Panmure House, which still stands.

2. James Boswell (1740-1795)

Born in Edinburgh, the son of Lord Auchinleck, a judge, he came from an ancient Ayrshire family. Perhaps in reaction to his strict upbringing, young Boswell became something of a rake, and his very full and frank journals disclose explicit details of his amatory and drinking exploits. While in London in 1763 he met Dr Samuel Johnson (1709-1784), and his *Life of Samuel Johnson* (1791) is still considered one of the greatest biographies ever written. In 1773 Boswell persuaded Johnson to embark on a tour of Scotland and the Hebrides, and both men published entertaining and observant accounts of their travels. Boswell practised with indifferent success at the Scottish Bar, and had a flat in James Court off the Lawnmarket, where he entertained Johnson during his trip to Scotland.

3. Voltaire (1694-1778)

Except, of course, that he said it in French! However, Voltaire's words show the extent to which Scotland, and especially Edinburgh, had become recognised across Europe as a primary centre for all sorts of intellectual enquiry – truly a 'hotbed of genius'.

4. David Hume (1711-1776)

Scotland's greatest philosopher, and one of the greatest of all time, Hume's radical scepticism and empiricism led to his work being coolly received at the time, and to his reputation – possibly undeserved – as an out-and-out atheist (the main reason that he never secured a position at any of Scotland's universities). He was, however, a sociable man of great amiability and a close friend of many of the leading lights of the Enlightenment, including Adam Smith. Cooking was one of his favourite pastimes, and he enjoyed little more than preparing meals for his friends.

5. In the pub!

Before the general move to the New Town, even the wealthy often lived in tiny cramped apartments, and the Old Town's many taverns were where people socialised, debated and carried out their business. Enlightenment intellectuals belonged, generally, to several of the city's many clubs that met regularly in favourite taverns to discuss the latest ideas over a glass of claret, a pipe of tobacco and a dish of oysters. They were not just great thinkers, but great drinkers too!

6. Robert Fergusson (1750-1774)

This brilliant young poet died at the early age of 24 in Edinburgh's insane asylum, where he had been committed after incurring a serious head injury in a fall. He was probably suffering from depression. Despite his short life, he left a legacy of brilliant poetry, mainly in Scots, including his masterpiece *Auld Reikie*. Robert Burns never met Fergusson, but was greatly influenced by his work, and when he learned that he was buried in a pauper's grave in Canongate Kirkyard paid for a suitable memorial to be erected. The epitaph, written by Burns, reads:

> No sculptur'd Marble here nor pompous lay
> No storied Urn nor animated Bust
> This simple Stone directs Pale Scotia's Way
> To pour her Sorrows o'er her Poet's Dust

In the 1890s Robert Louis Stevenson intended to pay for the tomb's restoration, but died before the work was completed. Fergusson is now also commemorated by a statue outside the entrance to Canongate Kirk, erected in 2004.

7. James Hutton (1726-1797)

A Berwickshire farmer by birth, he became fascinated by geology at an early age. His study of rock formations, not least at Salisbury Crags in Edinburgh, convinced him, in the face of established opinion, that the earth was immeasurably old – or as he memorably put it: 'We find no vestige of a beginning, no prospect of an end'. He is justly considered the father of modern geology.

8. Joseph Black (1728-1799)

A physician and scientist, Black was educated at both Glasgow and Edinburgh Universities. He became a professor at Glasgow in 1757, before moving to Edinburgh in 1766. His discovery of latent heat is the foundation of the modern science of thermodynamics; he also discovered carbon dioxide, which he called 'fixed air'.

9. William Robertson (1721-1793)

The minister of Greyfriars Kirk and Moderator of the General Assembly in 1763, Robertson was also an insightful historian, notably of Scotland and Spain. In 1762 he became Principal of Edinburgh University, a post he held until his death. It has been claimed that, 'The thirty years during which he presided over the University perhaps represent the highest point in its history'.

10. James Burnett, Lord Monboddo (1714-1799)

A judge eccentric even by the standards of the contemporary Scottish Bench, Lord Monboddo was also a considerable scholar and theorist, particularly in the field of linguistics. An early proponent of the idea of evolution, his comment about human tails attracted widespread ridicule, and he later retracted it.

ROUND 7

Military Edinburgh

Edinburgh is dominated by the brooding presence of the castle – for centuries the greatest fortress in Scotland, serving as a constant reminder that warfare and the military have always been at the centre of the city's story. Are you ready for the melee?

1. Which building, dedicated in 1927, commemorates Scotland's sacrifice in the Great War, and where can it be found?

2. Was Edinburgh bombed during the First World War?

3. Before the restructuring of the Scottish regiments in 2006, which regiment was particularly associated with Edinburgh, and what was its precedence in the British Army's order of battle?

4. At which battle near Edinburgh did Bonnie Prince Charlie's Jacobite army rout a force of Government redcoats in September 1745?

5. In which year did a Scottish force led by Thomas Randolph, Earl of Moray, recapture Edinburgh Castle from the English?

   a. 1312
   b. 1313
   c. 1314

6. Which English king ordered the total destruction of Edinburgh in 1544?

7. How many military museums are there in Edinburgh Castle, and can you name them?

8. What killed over 200 soldiers from Edinburgh in May 1915, hundreds of miles from the front line?

9. In which decade was Edinburgh Castle's Half Moon Battery built?

   a. 1470s
   b. 1570s
   c. 1670s

10. How many barracks are currently occupied by the City of Edinburgh Garrison?

I hope you survived that unwounded. The next round is a bit of a treasure hunt!

Answers – Round 7

1. The Scottish National War Memorial in Edinburgh Castle
Designed by the noted Scottish architect Sir Robert Lorimer,
this moving monument contains, apart from the central
shrine, individual memorials dedicated to each of the
famous Scottish regiments and to other branches of service
such as the Royal Navy and the RAF. In front of each memorial a Book of Honour records the names of the fallen, now
not just in the Great War but in the Second World War and
subsequent conflicts as well. To this day, whenever a Scottish
serviceman is killed on active service his name is added to
the relevant Book of Honour.

2. Yes
We tend to associate bombing with the Second World War
(and indeed Edinburgh was raided several times during that
conflict), but Edinburgh's first encounter with aerial bombardment came in April 1916 when two German Zeppelin
airships caused extensive damage in Leith and the city
centre. Thirteen people were killed and almost thirty injured.

3. The Royal Scots, the First of Foot

The oldest regiment in the British Army, the Royal Scots can trace its ancestry back to 1633. In 2006, when all the Scottish line infantry regiments were restructured into the Royal Regiment of Scotland, the Royal Scots amalgamated with the King's Own Scottish Borderers to form the Royal Scots Borderers, 1st Battalion the Royal Regiment of Scotland (1 SCOTS).

4. The Battle of Prestonpans

The Jacobite army had captured Edinburgh (though not the castle) bloodlessly on 16 September 1745. A few days later a Government force, commanded by Sir John Cope, disembarked at Dunbar and marched towards Edinburgh to confront the Jacobites. Prince Charlie led his forces to meet Cope, whom they encountered at Prestonpans a few miles to the east of the city. At dawn on the 21st of September battle was joined, when the Government forces rapidly broke in the face of a highland charge. This outcome greatly boosted Jacobite morale, and led to the decision a month later to invade England. However, the Jacobites were finally crushed bloodily at the Battle of Culloden near Inverness in April 1746.

5. c. 14 March 1314

However, a plaque in the castle records it as taking place in 1313! This difference arises because, until 1600, Scotland recognised 25 March as New Year's Day. As a result, 14 March 1313 (old style) became 14 March 1314 (new style).

6. Henry VIII

Henry was determined that the infant Mary Queen of Scots should marry his own son, later Edward VI. However, the Scots were generally unconvinced of the wisdom of this match, and so from 1543 to 'persuade' them Henry repeatedly ordered English armies to invade Scotland and cause as much devastation as they could. This period is known in Scottish history as 'The Rough Wooing'. In particular, in May 1544 an English army commanded by the Earl of Hertford took Edinburgh in pursuit of Henry's command to burn it to the ground. At that time most of the city was built of timber or wattle and daub, with thatched roofs. As a result, the only buildings to survive the English onslaught even partially were those built of stone.

7. Three

These are the regimental museums of the Royal Scots (see 3 above) and of the Royal Scots Dragoon Guards (Scotland's only cavalry regiment), together with the Scottish National War Museum. Entry to all these museums is free, once you have paid the admission charge to the castle.

8. The Quintinshill railway disaster, 22 May 1915

This is the worst accident in the history of British railways, resulting in the deaths of 226 people, of whom 215 were soldiers from 1/7th (Leith) Battalion the Royal Scots, who were being shipped to Gallipoli. The immediate cause of the disaster, which involved three trains colliding, was the inattention of the signalmen on duty at Quintinshill Signal Box, just on this side of the English border.

9. b. 1570s

After the forced abdication of Mary Queen of Scots in 1567, Edinburgh Castle was held by a garrison still loyal to the now deposed Queen, under the command of Sir William Kirkcaldy of Grange. After several years of stand-off and intermittent truces, the besieging forces sought help from Queen Elizabeth I of England. Consequently, an English army arrived in May 1573 and started bombarding the castle with heavy siege guns. Finally, after days of bombardment, the castle's main frontal defence, David's Tower, collapsed in rubble and the garrison surrendered. The Half Moon Battery, perhaps the castle's most prominent feature, was built on the ruins of David's Tower as part of the reconstruction of the defences following this 'lang siege'. As a sad footnote, Kirkcaldy of Grange, who had so gallantly held the castle for Queen Mary, was hanged in front of St Giles on the 3rd of August.

10. Three

These are Redford Barracks, home to 3rd Battalion the Rifles; Dreghorn Barracks home to the Royal Scots Borderers (1 SCOTS); and Glencorse Barracks, home to the Royal Highland Fusiliers (2 SCOTS). In addition, the Edinburgh garrison still has its headquarters in Edinburgh Castle, although no regiment has been based there since the 1920s.

ROUND 8

Hidden Edinburgh

Looking up and down and all around always pays off when exploring Edinburgh. Hidden gems and unexpected treasures can be found around many a corner. This round probes your curiosity and powers of observation.

1. What gives Cannonball House its name?

2. What is hidden beneath Edinburgh's City Chambers?

3. Where will you see the antlers of a stag shot on the Queen's Balmoral estate prominently displayed?

4. Where can you find a museum dedicated to the history of money?

5. Where is 'Heave Awa Hoose', and what is the reason for its strange name?

6. Who is buried under car parking space 23 in Parliament Square?

7. Where on the Royal Mile will you find a garden laid out in seventeenth-century style?

8. Which First World War commander is commemorated by a plaque in Charlotte Square and a statue in Edinburgh Castle?

9. Where is there a temple to Hygeia, the Roman goddess of health?

10. Where will you find a statue of Tubal-Cain, the metal worker mentioned in Genesis 4.22?

Did you manage to find everything? If not, you're about to be punished!

Answers - Round 8

1. A cannonball lodged in its west gable facing the castle
Cannonball House sits at the foot of the Castle Esplanade, and dates from the early seventeenth century. There are various stories of how the cannonball got there. The most romantic says that during the Jacobite occupation of the city in 1745 a gun was fired down the Royal Mile from the castle, and the ball struck and became lodged in the house. Others say that it was added in Victorian times as a wily piece of tourism PR. The more prosaic truth is probably that it was carefully inserted here by engineers to mark the height above sea level of the spring at Comiston, to the south of the city, which provided Edinburgh with its first piped supply of fresh water in the 1620s.

2. Mary King's Close
This seventeenth-century street was built over when the present City Chambers were constructed in the 1750s, and the resulting subterranean warren is now a popular visitor attraction. In 1645 plague struck the city, and there are legends of the inhabitants being bricked up there to prevent it spreading. This is not actually true, but the Close is widely reputed to be haunted, and visiting it remains an eerie experience.

3. On top of the gable of the Canongate Kirk

Displayed here are the arms of the former Burgh of Canongate which comprise a gilded stag's head with a cross rising between its antlers, in reference to the foundation legend of Holyrood Abbey (see Round 4, question 2). The stag's antlers are real, and come from a stag shot on the Balmoral Estate.

4. The Museum on the Mound

Based in the Bank of Scotland's headquarters building at the top of the Mound, this fascinating small museum tells the story of money from the earliest times, and covers the history of the Bank of Scotland. Like nearly all Edinburgh museums, admission is free.

5. Paisley Close on High Street

By Victorian times the Old Town had largely become an overcrowded slum, as the wealthier citizens had moved to the New Town. In November 1861, an ancient sixteenth-century tenement on this site suddenly collapsed, killing thirty-five of its occupants and trapping many more in the rubble. A young man, Joseph McIvor, was among those trapped, and as the rescuers frantically sought to free him he cried out, 'Heave awa, chaps. I'm no dead yet!' McIvor's bust is now carved above the lintel to Paisley Close along with the words he shouted to encourage his rescuers. This appalling disaster led directly to the City Improvement Act of 1867, under which many of the Old Town's more festering slums were cleared.

6. John Knox

The great Reformer, for many years the minister of St Giles, was buried here in 1572, in what used to be the old St Giles burying ground before Parliament House was built in the 1630s.

7. Dunbar's Close

Off the Canongate, just below the Canongate Kirk, the narrow entrance to Dunbar's Close takes you into a hidden delight. This secluded haven was reclaimed from wilderness in 1978 and laid out in the style and character of a seventeenth-century garden. It offers superb views across to Calton Hill.

8. Earl Haig (1861-1928)

Field Marshall Sir Douglas Haig, later Earl Haig, was the British Commander-in-Chief on the Western Front from 1915 to 1918. He was born in a house on the south side of Charlotte Square, now marked by a plaque, and his equestrian statue can be found in front of the Scottish National War Museum in the castle. For eighty-five years the statue stood on the Castle Esplanade, but it was relocated in 2009 in order to accommodate new, larger spectator stands for the Military Tattoo each August.

9. St Bernard's Well on the Water of Leith,
    between Dean Village and Stockbridge

The water from the natural spring here was reputed to be excellent for the health, and in 1789 the artist Alexander Naismith was commissioned to design this little circular temple, based on the Temple of Vesta at Tivoli. Under the dome is a statue of Hygeia, the Greek goddess of health (from which we get our word 'hygiene').

10. Nicolson Square

The statue of Tubal-Cain sits atop a column originally erected by the Brassmakers' Guild of Edinburgh for the International Exhibition held in the Meadows in 1886.

Crime and Punishment in Edinburgh

Like all ancient cities, Edinburgh has a darker side. I hope you're not squeamish, as we are about to delve into its criminal annals and some of the more unpleasant punishments meted out in the past.

1. 'Up the close and doon the stair, But an ben wi Burke and Hare'. To what notorious crimes does this street rhyme refer?

2. By what name is HM Prison Edinburgh generally known?

3. What does the Witches' Well commemorate?

4. Why would you not want to become too acquainted with Edinburgh's Maiden?

5. The World's End is a popular Royal Mile pub. What infamous connotation did the name acquire in the 1970s?

6. When did Edinburgh's last public execution take place?

7. Which pioneering Edinburgh detective published his sensational memoirs in the 1860s, and has more recently been the hero of a long-running series of radio dramas?

8. Why is Major Weir notorious?

9. Why would you not want to wear the Boot in seventeenth-century Edinburgh?

10. What macabre crime took place in Queensberry House (now part of the Scottish Parliament complex) on the very day the Act of Union was signed in 1707?

That wasn't too painful, was it? The next round takes us back to long, long ago.

Answers - Round 9

1. **A series of sixteen murders committed in 1828 by two Irishmen, William Burke and William Hare**

At this time Edinburgh was Europe's leading centre for medical education, resulting in an insatiable demand for cadavers for anatomical dissection. Bodysnatchers (or 'resurrectionists') regularly raided Edinburgh's graveyards for freshly buried corpses to sell to the anatomists. Burke and Hare ran a lodging house in the West Port, and after one of their lodgers died of dropsy they sold the body to Dr Robert Knox, one of the leading anatomists. They saw here an opportunity for easy money and over the next ten months suffocated a total of sixteen lodgers, selling the bodies to Knox. When their crimes eventually came to light, Hare turned King's Evidence in exchange for immunity and Burke alone was hanged. Ironically, perhaps, his own corpse was then sold for dissection.

2. **Saughton, after the area of Edinburgh in which it stands**

Saughton Prison opened in 1924, replacing the old Calton Gaol that stood on the present site of St Andrew's House on Calton Hill.

3. **The site where around 300 witches were burned at the stake in the sixteenth and seventeenth centuries**

Accusations of witchcraft almost invariably led to conviction, and over this period as many as 3,000 people - mainly women - are believed to have been tortured and burned at the stake in Scotland. Edinburgh saw more of these horrific executions than anywhere else, and the Witches' Well stands at the site where most of them took place, at the foot of the Castle Esplanade. The Well itself is a small cast-iron drinking fountain, in art nouveau style, and was designed by John Duncan RSA. It was erected in 1911.

4. Because you were about to be beheaded!
The Maiden was a beheading machine, an early precursor of the guillotine, which came into use in Edinburgh in 1564 during the reign of Mary Queen of Scots. It was last used in 1716, by which time it had executed some 150 people. The grisly mechanism survives, and can be seen in the National Museum of Scotland.

5. The World's End Murders
In October 1977 two teenage girls, Christine Eadie and Helen Scott, were last seen alive leaving the pub at closing time. The following day their bound and naked bodies were found six miles apart in the countryside. For many years the crimes remained unsolved, but in 2007, following advances in DNA science, Angus Sinclair, already a convicted murderer and rapist, was charged with the murders. He was controversially acquitted on a legal technicality, and the ensuing public outrage led to a change in Scotland's law of 'Double Jeopardy'. Sinclair was tried again in 2014, and this time convicted of the murder of the two girls.

6. 21 June 1864
George Bryce, the 'Ratho Murderer', had been convicted of the brutal murder of a young woman at Ratho on the outskirts of Edinburgh, and was sentenced to hang. So notorious was his crime that thousands gathered to witness his execution,

which took place at the corner of Lawnmarket and George IV Bridge. Unfortunately, the hangman had miscalculated the length of rope needed for the drop and a quick death. As a result, the appalled crowd witnessed Bryce's slow and agonising strangulation – by some accounts it took 40 minutes for him to die. Such was the public revulsion that the city magistrates decided that all future executions would take place in private, in a special cell in Calton Gaol. The following year saw the last ever public execution in Scotland, on Glasgow Green.

7. James McLevy (1796–1875)

Originally from Northern Ireland, McLevy joined the Edinburgh Police in 1830. In 1833 he became the city's first detective, and over the next thirty years secured over 2,000 convictions. After retiring in the 1860s he published a popular series of books recording highlights of his career which are believed to have helped inspire Sir Arthur Conan Doyle's Sherlock Holmes stories. More recently, the BBC has broadcast several radio dramas based on McLevy's career, starring Brian Cox as the detective.

8. He was a warlock, executed for witchcraft

Major Thomas Weir (1599–1670) was a zealous Presbyterian who preached a particularly strict form of Calvinism. In 1650 he became commander of Edinburgh's Town Guard, hence his military rank. He lived in the West Bow with his sister Grizel and was, to all appearances, one of the city's most respected citizens. In 1670, already an old man, he spontaneously confessed to a life of unspeakable crime and debauchery, and to having long since sold his soul to the Devil. At first his confessions were not believed, but he persisted, and his story was fully corroborated by his sister. He was strangled and burnt at the stake on the road between Edinburgh and Leith. His sister shared his fate, being executed in the Grassmarket. Weir is a central character in *The Fanatic* by contemporary Scottish novelist James Robertson.

9. It was an instrument of torture

The Boot was a metal casing that was fastened tightly around the victim's lower leg. Wooden wedges were then hammered down into the space between the casing and the leg, causing intense pain and frequently splintering the bones of the leg. Sufferers were generally left crippled afterwards. It was used to extract confessions, notably from Covenanters (dissenting strict Presbyterians) in the 1670s and '80s.

10. Murder and cannibalism

James, Earl of Drumlanrig (1697-1715) was the eldest son of the Duke of Queensberry, the Government's principal agent in securing the passage of the Act of Union in 1707. Unfortunately, young Drumlanrig was violently insane, as well as being of quite exceptional strength for his age. He was kept locked up in a darkened room in Queensberry House (still to be seen at the foot of the Canongate). While the Act of Union was being signed, Edinburgh broke out in riot against the deeply unpopular Treaty. Perhaps taking advantage of the uproar, Drumlanrig somehow broke free. Seizing a young kitchen lad, he impaled him on the kitchen spit and proceeded to roast him over the fire. When discovered, he had already devoured parts of the unfortunate boy. Some said that this was divine judgement on Queensberry for his betrayal of the Scottish nation by forcing through the Union.

ROUND 10

Ancient Edinburgh

Edinburgh was awarded its charter as a Royal Burgh by King David I in the 1120s, but the record of human habitation within and around the city limits dates back many thousands of years before that. Here we head way back in time.

1. True or false: Edinburgh is named after the Northumbrian king Edwin, and simply means 'Edwin's fort'.

2. Did the Roman army have a fort on Edinburgh Castle Rock?

3. To which period do the earliest finds (so far) in Edinburgh Castle date?

   a. Neolithic
   b. Bronze Age
   c. Iron Age

4. Which tribe occupied the Edinburgh area when the Romans arrived in Scotland?

5. Where in Edinburgh can you see Iron Age cultivation terraces with the naked eye?

6. What is (probably) the oldest site of Christian worship in Edinburgh still in use?

7. Which suburb contains the oldest evidence of human presence in Edinburgh?

8. What ancient monument lies within the perimeter of Edinburgh Airport?

9. What remarkable find was made in 2001 in an Iron Age burial mound at Newbridge, on the outskirts of Edinburgh?

10. What ancient poem contains the earliest literary reference to Edinburgh?

*Back to the present day now, and I think
it's time for a breath of fresh air.*

Answers - Round 10

1. False

Edinburgh did indeed become part of the Anglo-Saxon Kingdom of Northumbria in the seventh century, and Edwin was one of the early Northumbrian kings. However, Edwin died around fifteen years before Edinburgh was captured by the Northumbrians, probably in 638. More importantly, the ancient Brittonic Celtic name 'Eidyn' is known to date back to before the Northumbrian occupation, while the hillfort on the Castle Rock was called Din Eidyn (Fort of Eidyn) by AD 600 at the latest. Evidently the Northumbrians merely translated the Celtic name into Old English as 'Edinburh'. Interestingly, the modern Gaelic name for the city, Dun Eideann, derives directly from the old British name Din Eidyn.

2. No

There is no evidence of a Roman presence on the Castle Rock, although they did have an important fort within the present city limits at Cramond on the banks of the Forth. There was also a Roman fort at Inveresk in East Lothian, about 10 miles from the city centre.

3. b. Bronze Age

Excavations in the 1990s uncovered evidence of late Bronze Age settlement around 850 BC. It is not yet known if a human presence was continuous thereafter, but if it was this would make Edinburgh Castle the longest continuously inhabited site in Scotland.

4. The Votadini

This Iron Age tribe occupied the south east of Scotland, including the Edinburgh area. Their main tribal capital was at Traprain Law in East Lothian, but they certainly occupied the site of Edinburgh Castle, as well as a hillfort on Arthur's Seat. The Votadini maintained generally friendly relations with the Romans, acting as something of a buffer state, if not a client kingdom.

5. Arthur's Seat

Iron Age cultivation terraces can be clearly seen on the hillside from the Duddingston direction.

6. St Cuthbert's Church

St Cuthbert's nestles under the western precipice of the Castle Rock, set back from Lothian Road, and it is believed that a church was founded on this site by St Cuthbert himself in the seventh century. Until the foundation of St Giles in the early twelfth century, this was the only parish church in Edinburgh, and it has some claim to be the oldest continuously existing parish in Scotland. The present building, of course, is a far cry from the wattle and daub structure that St Cuthbert would have known, and dates from the 1890s, though the spire was built as part of the previous church in 1790.

7. Cramond

Evidence was uncovered in the 1990s of an encampment of hunter-gatherers in Cramond dating back to about 8,500 BC. Until recently this was thought possibly to be the oldest evidence of human presence in Scotland, but in 2014 archaeologists found remains of stone tools near Biggar in Lanarkshire dating back to around 12,000 BC.

8. The Catstane

This is an upright standing stone that appears to have been originally raised in the Bronze Age as part of a burial complex. Subsequently it was re-used in the Iron Age, and bears a fragmentary Latin inscription dating from the fifth or sixth centuries AD, when the area was part of the territory of the Votadini (see 4 above). The inscription has been translated as: *In this tomb lies Vetta the daughter of Victricus.*

9. A chariot burial

This was uncovered by excavations in 2001, in advance of construction of a major road interchange. Radiocarbon dating revealed that the chariot was made between 475 and 380 BC, making it the oldest chariot burial in Britain. In 2007 a reconstruction of the chariot was made for the National Museum of Scotland.

10. Y Gododdin

This poem in Old Welsh tells the tale of the heroes of the Gododdin, the people previously known as the Votadini (see 4 above). Although the oldest manuscript dates from the thirteenth century, linguistic evidence leads many scholars to date the work to the early seventh century, virtually contemporary with the events it describes. The poem tells how, around AD 600, the king of the Gododdin, Mynyddog Mwynfawr, gathered 300 of his bravest warriors in his seat of Din Eidyn (Edinburgh Castle) and feasted them there for a whole year before leading them south to confront the Anglo-Saxons at 'Catraeth', believed to be modern Catterick in Yorkshire. There almost all of them were killed, facing overwhelming odds. It is instructive that not long afterwards Edinburgh became part of Anglo-Saxon Northumbria, and the Gododdin vanish from the pages of history.

ROUND 11

Green Edinburgh

Edinburgh is a compact city, yet within its limits are well over 100 public parks and gardens, together with thousands of private gardens and allotments. From an elevated position like the castle, one can look out on sweeping cascades of greenery in all directions. Let's spend some time strolling through these green spaces, the lungs that let the city breathe.

1. Which beautiful park, now in its fourth location, is a major centre for the scientific study of plants?

2. Why is Starbank Park so called?

3. Where is the Floral Clock?

4. Which park contains two of Edinburgh's most prominent landscape features, and yet is not managed by the City Council?

5. Which hill contains several iconic monuments and offers stunning views of both the Old and New Towns?

6. Which is the only Edinburgh park where horse riding is permitted?

7. Which park, now containing a pitch and putt course, was the mustering point for the Scottish army before the ill-fated Flodden campaign of 1513?

8. Which popular park, first laid out in the eighteenth century, has connections with the family of Robert Burns?

9. Which monarch has three Edinburgh parks named after him?

10. How many Natural Heritage Sites does Edinburgh contain?

Feeling refreshed? Now we'll return to the city centre.

Answers - Round 11

1. The Royal Botanic Garden

First established near Holyrood Palace in 1670, it moved in 1676 to a larger site now covered by platform 11 of Waverley Station. After a further transfer to a site off Leith Walk in 1763, it finally moved to its present location at Inverleith in 1820. Although a beautiful place to stroll through and a major visitor attraction for locals and tourists alike, the Garden is primarily a scientific institution, devoted to the study and conservation of plants from around the world.

2. It has a flower bed in the shape of a star on the side of a steep bank

This small park between Newhaven and Granton commands stunning views over the Firth of Forth to the Fife shore on the other side. The eight-pointed star represents the points of the compass, and relates to the river's seagoing heritage, when mariners from the Forth sailed all over the globe navigating by the stars.

3. West Princes Street Gardens, at the entrance from the foot of the Mound

The Floral Clock was first planted in 1903, and contains around 40,000 bedding plants in an ornate design whose theme is changed each summer. The present clock mechanism was installed in 1934.

4. Holyrood Park

This huge park, containing both Arthur's Seat and the Salisbury Crags, is a Royal Park now managed by Historic Environment Scotland. Historically associated with the Palace of Holyroodhouse, it is open to the public. A major route, Queen's Drive, runs through the park to Duddingston Village, while a loop road takes you much of the way up to the top of Arthur's Seat. Most of it is closed to vehicles on Sunday.

5. Calton Hill

This commanding hill just beyond the east end of Princes Street contains many of Edinburgh's most significant monuments, including the National Monument, the Nelson Monument, the Political Martyrs Monument and the City Observatory. The views over the city are outstanding in every direction, and it is a favourite spot from which to take photographs of Edinburgh.

6. Braid Hills

Rising to a height of 675 feet to the south of the city, this park offers spectacular views on all sides. Containing areas of urban forest, Braid Hills Park is popular with walkers and cyclists as well as with golfers using its two 18-hole courses.

7. Bruntsfield Links

This open park, to the south-west of the city centre, is all that remains of the former Burgh Muir. It was a traditional mustering point for Scottish armies, most notably before James IV's disastrous Flodden campaign in 1513, which resulted in the deaths of the king, much of the Scottish nobility and at least 5,000 other Scots. It was one of the earliest places where golf was played in Scotland (along with Leith Links), probably from the fifteenth century. The Bruntsfield Links Golfing Society, founded in 1761, is the fourth oldest golf club in the world, though it moved to a new course out of the city centre in the 1870s. The park still contains a short hole pitch-and-putt course, which is free to play, so maintains its ancient golfing associations.

8. The Meadows

This large park to the south of the Old Town is one of Edinburgh's most popular and important open spaces. It used to be the site of the Burgh Loch, but in the eighteenth century this was drained and landscaped. Among the gardeners working on the landscaping was William Burnes (1721-1784), the father of the poet Robert.

9. George V

Three Edinburgh parks, in Currie, Eyre Place, and South Queensferry, were named after George V to mark the king's death in 1936.

10. Twelve

Edinburgh's officially designated Natural Heritage Sites are managed by the city's Natural Heritage Service, assisted by enthusiastic volunteers.

ROUND 12

Buildings of Edinburgh

Edinburgh owes its beauty not only to its dramatic setting and natural landscapes but also to the outstanding quality of its architecture and urban planning, reflected by both the Old and New Towns forming a UNESCO World Heritage Site. Despite the occasional ravages of the developer, the integrity of the city's built environment has been preserved largely intact. Let's take a closer look.

1. What modern building sits at the foot of the Canongate, opposite the Royal Palace?

2. What is the name given to the smooth, finely cut masonry that faces most of the buildings in the New Town and many in the Old Town?

3. What is unusual about the form of St Andrew's and St George's West Church in George Street?

4. Which famous Scottish architect was responsible for both Register House and Charlotte Square, at opposite ends of the original New Town.

5. Which two features of the Scottish National Portrait Gallery in Queen Street are unusual for the New Town?

6. Which renowned architect designed both the Royal Scottish Academy and the National Gallery at the foot of the Mound?

7. The Great Hall of Edinburgh Castle and the crown spire on the tower of St Giles Cathedral were both built in the reign of which Scottish king?

8. When did the Palace of Holyroodhouse acquire its present form?

9. Why is the layout of the Canongate Kirk, built in the late seventeenth century, unusual for a church of this period?

10. Which late seventeenth-century development at the top of the Lawnmarket is now a hall of residence for Edinburgh University?

After that, it's time for a party!

Answers - Round 12

1. The Scottish Parliament

Completed in 2004, this controversial building was designed by the Spanish architect Enric Miralles. Apart from its challenging form, the building's construction was dogged by scandal. Delays (it was three years behind schedule) and cost overruns (the eventual cost of £414m compares with an initial estimate of £40m) resulted in a public enquiry, which revealed an embarrassing lack of control and expertise in the management of the project. Individuals must decide for themselves whether they approve of the finished product.

2. Ashlar

This term is used to describe smoothly cut, close fitting blocks of masonry, and contrasts with the 'rubble' construction seen in much of the Old Town, and the deliberate 'rustication' used for decorative effect in many New Town buildings.

3. It is elliptical in form

St Andrew's, as it was originally called, was the first church to be built in the New Town, opening in 1784. Designed by Captain Andrew Frazer of the Royal Engineers, its unusual shape was probably to accommodate the shallow site on which it was built, although there is a story that it is so the Devil can't find any corners to hide in. (Unkind Englishmen say it is so that Scotsmen can't hide when they pass round the collection plate!) Renowned for its fine acoustics and its slim lofty spire, it was the scene of the Great Disruption in 1843 (see Round 4, question 9). In 1964 the congregation merged with that of St George's Church in Charlotte Square, which is now the home of West Register House.

4. Robert Adam (1728-1792)
A pioneer of neo-classicism, Kirkcaldy-born Adam was the son of one renowned architect (William) and the brother of another (John). Distinguished also as an interior designer, Adam is reckoned to be one of the greatest architects of the eighteenth century. Much of his practice was south of the border, but in Edinburgh, apart from Register House and Charlotte Square, he designed the Old College of the University on South Bridge.

5. It is built of red sandstone and in the gothic revival style
Nearly all the New Town is built of the local blonde sandstone and in classical Georgian style, so this massive red gothic structure stands out starkly. Completed in 1889, the building was designed by Rowand Anderson, and paid for entirely by John Ritchie Findlay (1824-1898), the proprietor of *The Scotsman* newspaper.

6. William Playfair (1790-1857)
Playfair was one of the greatest Scottish architects of the nineteenth century, responsible among much else for two of Edinburgh's finest and most prominent neo-classical buildings, the Royal Scottish Academy (completed in 1828) and the National Gallery (completed in 1859), both at the foot of the Mound.

7. James IV

A true Renaissance prince, James IV is perhaps the most charismatic and attractive of the Stewart kings. Until his untimely death in 1513 at Flodden Field (see Round 11, question 7), he was a great patron of the arts as well as being an inveterate builder. He ordered the construction of the present Great Halls at both Edinburgh and Stirling Castles and had the open crown spire added to the tower of St Giles as a symbol of imperial monarchy. Completed around the year 1500, this has been one of Edinburgh's most conspicuous landmarks for over 500 years.

8. Between 1671 and 1678

Following the Restoration of the Monarchy in 1660, Charles II ordered the reconstruction of Holyrood Palace, which had been badly damaged during the Cromwellian interregnum. The work was entrusted to Sir William Bruce and Robert Mylne, the King's Master Mason in Scotland. Cleverly, they mirrored the existing sixteenth-century north-west tower with a matching tower to the south-west, connecting the two with a grand screen topped by the Royal Arms of Scotland and an octagonal cupola. Behind this screen, the palace runs round three sides of the central courtyard.

9. It is cruciform in shape

Before the Reformation in the sixteenth century, nearly all major churches had a cruciform (cross-shaped) layout, with the long arm, on an east-west alignment, forming the nave and choir. The short arms provided transepts to north and south of the crossing. With the change in religious practice after the Reformation, where the emphasis was now on the preaching of God's Word, this layout went out of use. It is therefore highly unusual in Scotland to have a Protestant church of this period (the late seventeenth century) built to a cruciform plan.

10. Milne's Court

In 1690 the King's Master Mason Robert Mylne (see 8 above) built Milne's Court (note the different spelling!) as a speculative venture to provide upmarket housing. It was then revolutionary to build round the four sides of an open court, as opposed to the much more congested layout typical of the rest of the Old Town. Beautifully restored from 1969 to 1970, it now provides the most characterful halls of residence in the city, accommodating 176 of Edinburgh University's students.

ROUND 13

Festival Edinburgh

Every summer, mostly in August, Edinburgh plays host to an artistic feast as a whole swathe of cultural festivals are held in the city. Collectively these form the largest arts festival in the world, and for a month the apparently demure city lifts its skirts and kicks its knees up as it is flooded with performers and visitors from around the globe. Are you in carnival mood? If so, join me as we explore the ins and outs of Festival Edinburgh.

1. Which spectacular event has taken place on the Esplanade of the castle every August since 1950?

2. In what year was the Edinburgh International Festival first held?

3. Why is the 'Fringe' so called?

4. How many performances took place during the 2015 Festival Fringe?

   a. over 30,000
   b. over 40,000
   c. over 50,000

5. What event takes place every August in Charlotte Square Gardens?

6. What is the principal venue for classical music concerts during the International Festival?

7. How does Edinburgh mark the end of the Festival each year?

8. What sort of performance is particularly associated with the Pleasance?

9. Which of Edinburgh's festivals is normally held in October?

10. And which one in June?

Now that you're properly cultured,
how about some sea air?

Answers - Round 13

1. The Royal Edinburgh Military Tattoo

The Tattoo is a magical combination of splendid military precision, rousing martial music and colourful theatricality. The British armed forces predominate, but each year's programme involves many performers from around the world. Every performance begins with the massed pipes and drums of the Scottish regiments, joined by pipe bands from other countries, marching out of the Castle Gatehouse and fanning out onto the Esplanade in a swirl of tartan. A highlight towards the end of the show is when a lone piper appears floodlit high on the castle ramparts and plays a lament. The audience sits in temporary stands which start to be erected in May each year and are dismantled after the final performance. These stands seat around 9,500 people for each show, which is performed every weeknight and twice on Saturdays (no Sunday performances) during its three-week run. The Tattoo is normally sold out well in advance, but millions more watch it on television, where it is broadcast to some thirty countries.

2. 1947

The International Festival was the inspiration of Sir Rudolf Bing, an Austrian-born opera impresario and one of Edinburgh's civic leaders. After six long years of war, it was conceived as an international celebration of the performing arts to lift the spirits of a war-weary Scotland, Britain and Europe with cultural performances of the highest standard. The 'official' Festival, as it is often called, focuses on performances by world-class orchestras, opera and theatre companies. Since 1999 the Festival's central booking office and information centre has been based in The Hub, the former Tolbooth Church on Castlehill.

3. Originally because it was on the 'fringe'
of the International Festival

In 1947, the first year of the International Festival, eight theatre companies that did not form part of the official programme turned up in Edinburgh, performing in small unconventional venues as the main theatres and concert halls were all being used by the main Festival. The Fringe has grown year-on-year, and now dwarfs the official Festival in the number (though not always the quality) of performers and performances. True to its origins, it remains an open access festival – anyone can register through the organising Fringe Society and put on any show they want. This lack of any form of quality control can make buying a ticket for a show something of a lottery: some are of outstanding quality, others less so. The Fringe is now dominated by stand-up comedy, which since 2008 has comprised the majority of performances.

4. *c.* Over 50,000

The 2015 Fringe featured 50,459 performances of 3,314 different shows in 313 venues across the city, while ticket sales totalled almost £2.3m, making it by far the largest arts festival in the world.

5. The Edinburgh International Book Festival

Launched in 1983, it is one of the largest literary festivals in the world. World-renowned writers come to talk about their latest books, and there is an intense programme of cultural discussion and debate. Events are run especially for children, and there is a large temporary bookshop. For the month of August, the green lawns of Charlotte Square disappear under a forest of white marquees, where the various events take place.

6. The Usher Hall

Completed in 1914, this large circular building, topped by a distinctive shallow dome, has been Edinburgh's main concert hall ever since. Its construction was funded by whisky magnate Andrew Usher, and it can seat 2,200 people in the auditorium, which is renowned for its outstanding acoustics. A major refurbishment was completed in 2009.

7. By a fireworks display and concert

This spectacular display is launched from the ramparts of the castle and lasts around 45 minutes. The fireworks are choreographed to match the accompanying music played by the Scottish Chamber Orchestra.

8. Stand-up comedy

As noted in 3 above, comedy is now the most common type of Fringe performance. The Pleasance is one of a number of major Fringe venues now chiefly devoted to comedy and cabaret. The Pleasance complex consists of a number of buildings around a central cobbled courtyard. Away from the Festival, the Pleasance is a student recreation complex owned by the University of Edinburgh.

9. The Scottish International Storytelling Festival

First held in 1989, this is a celebration of the art of storytelling and oral traditions from around the world. The main venue is the Storytelling Centre's Netherbow Theatre, adjacent to John Knox House on the Royal Mile, although other venues around the city are also used.

10. The Edinburgh International Film Festival

The Film Festival started in 1947, the same year as the International Festival. It used to be held in August, along with the other main festivals, but was moved to late June in 2008.

ROUND 14

Maritime Edinburgh

We don't often think of Edinburgh as a seaside town, but stand on the Castle Esplanade and look at the New Town sweeping steeply down to the Firth of Forth, with views across to the hills of Fife; or look down the length of the Royal Mile to the coastline of East Lothian in the distance. In fact, the city has many miles of coastline within its modern limits, and its maritime heritage is rich and eventful, centring on the bustling port of Leith. It's time for a walk along the waterfront.

1. Where is Edinburgh's own beach resort?

2. Which organisation manages the Port of Leith?

3. Which river flows into the Forth at Cramond?

4. Why did the women of Newhaven regularly come into the centre of Edinburgh?

5. When did Leith finally become part of the City of Edinburgh?

6. Newhaven means 'new harbour'. When was it new?

7. Which foreign army garrisoned Leith in the 1550s?

8. Which famous person landed at Leith in 1561?

9. What sporting event used to take place on Leith Sands until 1816?

10. Where is the Scottish Merchant Navy Memorial?

After that short cruise, let's take in some sculpture.

Answers - Round 14

1. Portobello

Lying 3 miles east of the city centre on the Firth of Forth, Portobello has extensive, spacious sands and was developed as a beach resort in the second half of the nineteenth century. With the increasing popularity of foreign holidays, it went into something of a decline in the late twentieth century, but the twenty-first century has seen a considerable recovery in its fortunes. It is a popular place for a family day out on sunny days, has many attractive bars and restaurants, and offers one of the few Turkish baths remaining in Scotland. It was the birthplace of Sir Harry Lauder, the popular music hall performer. It owes its unusual name to the fact that a sailor who had served with the British fleet during the capture of Portobelo in Panama in 1739 built a cottage there, and named it 'Portobello Hut' to commemorate the victory.

2. Forth Ports Limited

As well as Leith, Forth Ports operates five other ports on the Forth, as well as Dundee on the Firth of Tay and Tilbury on the Thames.

3. The Almond

Running for 28 miles from North Lanarkshire through West Lothian before reaching the Forth at Cramond, the River Almond flows through areas that used to be dominated by heavy industry and mining. As a result it became heavily polluted, but with the decline of these traditional industries in the last fifty years it is now much cleaner and has been strongly repopulated by wildlife.

4. To sell fish

Until the middle of the twentieth century, Newhaven was predominantly a fishing village. The Newhaven 'fishwives' used to come into the centre of the city carrying baskets of fresh fish on their backs, which they would sell in the streets. Their distinctive and picturesque attire made them popular subjects for early photography in the mid-nineteenth century. A popular Scots song by Lady Nairne refers to this (note that 'caller' means 'fresh'): *Wha'll buy my caller herrin, new drawn frae the Forth?*

5. 1920

Leith had been an independent burgh in its own right since 1833, but population growth meant that by the end of the nineteenth century Leith and Edinburgh formed one continuous urban area. By the Edinburgh Boundaries Extension Act of 1920, the city absorbed not only Leith but such suburbs as Cramond, Corstorphine, Gilmerton and Colinton. A plebiscite in Leith at the time rejected the Edinburgh takeover by more than 5 to 1, but it went ahead anyway. One suspects that many Leithers are still not reconciled to the fact!

6. 1504

King James IV was determined to make Scotland a major naval power, and to that end ordered the construction of what was, at the time, the largest and most powerful warship in Europe. Because of the size of the *Great Michael* (as she was called) a totally new dock had to be built to accommodate her construction, and this was called 'Newhaven'. The *Great Michael* was completed in 1512, but following the King's death at Flodden in 1513 she was sold to France in 1514.

7. The French Army

In response to the 'Rough Wooing' of the 1540s (see Round 7, question 6), French forces arrived to assist the Scots in 1548. During the religious and political turmoil of the 1550s leading up to the Reformation, these French troops from their base in Leith supported the efforts of the Regent Marie de Guise (mother of Mary Queen of Scots) to uphold the old religion. Following Marie's death and the official enactment of the Reformation in 1560, both French and English forces evacuated Scotland under the terms of the Treaty of Edinburgh.

8. Mary Queen of Scots

Mary had been brought up at the French court from an early age and married the Dauphin, heir to the French throne. For a year, Mary was Queen of both Scotland and France, but following the death of her young husband, Francis II of France, she determined to return to Scotland to take up her personal rule. She landed at Leith on the 19th of August 1561, but her ship had arrived earlier than expected, so there was no official welcoming party. Despite this inauspicious start, she was rapturously received by the Edinburgh crowd on her progress to Holyrood Palace. Her reign was, however, destined to be short and turbulent, and she was compelled to abdicate in favour of her infant son in 1567.

9. Horse racing

The Leith Races were one of the most popular annual festivals for the people of Edinburgh, a release from the cares of everyday life and an opportunity for the city to let down its hair, as vividly depicted in one of Robert Fergusson's most rambunctious poems. In 1816, however, the races were transferred to Musselburgh, where they remain to this day.

10. Tower Place, Leith

This striking stone and bronze memorial was unveiled by the Princess Royal in 2010, to commemorate the 6,500 Scottish merchant seamen who lost their lives in the two world wars. Sculpted by artist Jill Watson, it depicts vessels and scenes of military life from the age of sail to modern container ships. Fittingly, it stands by The Shore, the heart of the old port of Leith, and in front of the former Leith Sailors' home, now the Malmaison Hotel.

ROUND 15

Monumental Edinburgh

As you would expect of a capital city, Edinburgh abounds in monuments and statues to the great and good – and sometimes to the not so great or good! This round will test your memory for memorials.

1. Arguably Edinburgh's most loved and best-known statue is of an animal, not a human being. What does it portray?

2. Whose equestrian statue can be found in the centre of Charlotte Square?

3. Whose colossal image sits on top of the Royal Scottish Academy at the foot of the Mound?

4. Which monument carries a time signal, synchronised with the One O'Clock Gun?

5. Which monument is sometimes called 'Scotland's Disgrace'?

6. Where in Edinburgh will you find a statue of Abraham Lincoln?

7. Which is the oldest statue in Edinburgh?

8. A new statue was unveiled outside the National Museum in September 2016. Whom does it depict?

9. Where is the Scottish American War Memorial?

10. Where will you find a statue of former Prime Minister William Gladstone?

I hope you found that 'monumentally' interesting.
Let's take a trip to the next round.

Answers - Round 15

1. Greyfriars Bobby

This little statue of a Skye terrier sitting atop a granite column was erected in 1873. Bobby's master, an Edinburgh policeman, died in 1858 and was buried in the adjacent Greyfriars Kirkyard. Legend has it that the little dog refused to leave his master's grave except to be fed, and guarded it by day and night until he himself died in 1872. The people of Edinburgh took the wee dog to their hearts, so much so that when legislation was introduced in 1867 requiring dogs to be licenced the Lord Provost, Sir William Chambers, directed that the city should pay for Bobby's licence. Bobby became world-famous after an American lady, Eleanor Atkinson, wrote a short novel about him in 1912. In 1961 a Disney movie – which quite effectively recreates the atmosphere of mid-nineteenth-century Edinburgh – brought him further fame. Bobby himself was buried in Greyfriars near his master, and in 1981 a red granite tombstone was erected on his grave. It should be noted that over the last century several writers have cast doubt on some details of the traditional tale.

2. Prince Albert (1819-1861)

This statue of Queen Victoria's beloved husband was erected by public subscription in 1876. The statue was unveiled by the Queen herself, who was greatly moved by the occasion. On the same day she knighted the sculptor, Sir John Steell.

3. Queen Victoria

This huge stone statue of the young Queen Victoria was sculpted by Sir John Steell, and completed in 1844. Edinburgh's only other statue of the Queen, this time in her perhaps more familiar maturity, is at the foot of Leith Walk and was unveiled in 1907. It was sculpted by John Stephenson Rhind.

4. The Nelson Monument

This tall memorial tower to Admiral Lord Nelson was erected by public subscription in the aftermath of his great victory – and tragic death – at the Battle of Trafalgar in 1805, and was completed in 1815. With its position at the highest point of Calton Hill, it provides a dramatic termination to the view along Princes Street. As an appropriately nautical touch, the 105-foot high tower takes the form of an upturned telescope. Since 1853 the mast on top of the tower has held a time ball, which is hoisted to the top of the mast shortly before 1 p.m. each day. At the precise time that the One O'Clock Gun is fired from the ramparts of the castle (a tradition established in 1861), the ball is dropped to the foot of the mast. Both these time signals were originally instituted to enable ships in Leith to set their chronometers to Greenwich Mean Time.

5. The National Monument

This was built as Scotland's memorial to the Scottish soldiers and sailors who died during the Napoleonic Wars. The
original intention was to build a replica of the Parthenon,
but, after three years of construction, the money ran out
in 1829 – hence its unfortunate nickname of 'Scotland's
Disgrace'. Standing next to the Nelson Monument (see 4
above), it provides a further striking closure to the vista
along Princes Street.

6. Calton Old Burial Ground

The statue of Lincoln is the centrepiece of the American Civil
War Memorial, which was erected in 1893 to commemorate
the emancipation of the slaves as well as six Scots who died
fighting in the Civil War. It was the work of an American
sculptor, George Bissell, and the funds for its construction
were all raised in the United States.

7. The statue of Charles II in Parliament Square

This statue was completed a month before the King's
death in February 1685, but was not erected until shortly
afterwards as the plinth was not ready. Commissioned by
Edinburgh Town Council, it is made of lead supported on
an internal iron framework. It has required extensive restoration several times over the last three centuries, as the
supporting iron framework is prone to rust and buckling. The
most recent restoration was in 2011.

8. William Playfair (1790-1857)

See Round 12, question 6 for more information on Playfair.
This splendid new statue, funded by the National Museum,

the City Council and Edinburgh University, is by the renowned contemporary sculptor Alexander 'Sandy' Stoddart, who is the Queen's Sculptor in Ordinary in Scotland. Stoddart is also responsible for the statues of David Hume and Adam Smith on the Royal Mile, and that of the scientist James Clerk Maxwell in George Street.

9. West Princes Street Gardens

Also known as 'The Call', this memorial by the Canadian sculptor Robert Tait McKenzie was erected in 1927. The main figure is of a kilted young soldier looking towards the castle. He sits in front of a frieze depicting a procession of marching men, at the rear in civilian clothes, then in uniform, and finally led by a pipe band. The memorial was funded by Americans of Scottish blood to commemorate Scotland's extraordinary contribution in the Great War. A remembrance service is held there every year on the last Monday of May, American Memorial Day, organised by the English-Speaking Union Scotland. The US armed forces provide a guard of honour and colour party, while the British Army provides a military band and pipers. Each service is conducted by a distinguished Edinburgh clergyman.

10. Coates Crescent

William Ewart Gladstone (1809-1898) was one of the most distinguished British statesmen of the nineteenth century. Originally a Tory, he became a Liberal in the 1850s and served four times as Prime Minister. The statue with its attendant figures is by James Pittendrigh MacGillivray and was first erected in 1917. It originally stood in St Andrew Square and was moved to its present site in 1955.

ROUND 16

Transport in Edinburgh

All cities need effective means of transport to thrive. Got your ticket? Then hop aboard!

1. What controversial new transport system was inaugurated in May 2014?

2. Where is Edinburgh's oldest surviving railway station?

3. When was the Forth (Railway) Bridge opened?

4. When was the Forth Road Bridge opened?

5. What is the name of the new road bridge across the Forth, opened in 2017?

6. What was the main means of personal conveyance in Edinburgh before the New Town was built?

7. What new railway link did Edinburgh acquire in September 2015?

8. What is the name of Edinburgh's ring road?

9. By 1750 the Edinburgh Enlightenment was in full swing. How long did it take to travel from London to Edinburgh by stagecoach?

10. Why was Edinburgh's first railway nicknamed the 'Innocent Railway'?

That's it – you've arrived safely. Next we'll play some games.

Answers - Round 16

1. Edinburgh Trams

Edinburgh had an extensive tramway network from Victorian times until 1956, when it finally closed, but by the early twenty-first century plans for a new modern tram system were proposed. In 2006 the City Council obtained parliamentary approval for a scheme that would link Leith to the airport, running through the city centre, with a loop line from Haymarket to Granton. Construction started in 2008, but from the outset the project was bedevilled by delays, cost overruns and contractual disputes. In 2011 the extension to Leith and the branch to Granton were cancelled, and the truncated line, running for 9 miles from York Place to the airport, finally opened in May 2014, three years behind the original schedule. The disruption caused by construction, especially in the city centre, was a major source of annoyance and criticism for the people of Edinburgh, and the eventual cost of over £776m for the shortened route compares with an initial estimate for the whole project of £498m.

2. Haymarket

Opened in 1842, Haymarket was the original terminus of the Edinburgh and Glasgow Railway until the line was extended through Princes Street Gardens to Waverley in 1846. Haymarket saw almost 2.5 million passengers in 2014/15, and to improve passenger facilities a major reconstruction, including a new concourse, was completed in December 2013. The original station building is Category A listed, and has been preserved in the reconstructed station.

3. 1890

For almost 130 years the towering triple cantilever towers of the Forth Bridge have been an icon of Scotland, instantly recognised around the world. When completed, its 53,000 tonnes of steel, held together by about 6.5 million rivets, made it the largest steel structure in the world. Including the approach viaducts, it is over 1.5 miles long, the towers each rise to 330 feet above high water level, and there is over 150 feet of navigation clearance between the track bed and high water. On completion, it revolutionised transport links between Edinburgh and the north.

4. 1964

When opened by Her Majesty the Queen, this elegant 1.5-mile-long suspension bridge had the same revolutionary effect on road links to the north as the Forth Bridge had had on rail links seventy-four years earlier. It replaced a vehicular ferry service between the towns of North and South Queensferry that was notorious for its delays. Originally designed to carry 30,000 vehicles a day, it now regularly carries more than 60,000. This extra burden causes frequent traffic delays, while it has also impacted the integrity of the bridge's structure, resulting in a three-week closure of the bridge in December 2015 to enable remedial repairs to be carried out. Until 2008 a toll was charged for crossing the bridge, but this was abolished in February that year.

5. The Queensferry Crossing

The extra traffic flow across the Forth Road Bridge (see 4 above) led to a decision in 2007 to construct an additional road crossing of the Forth at Queensferry. Taking the form of a triple-towered cable-stayed bridge, at 1.7 miles long it is slightly longer than both the Forth Road Bridge and the Forth Bridge. Construction started in 2011, and with its opening in summer 2017 it has been completed more or less on time and to budget. Some say that this is sufficiently unusual for a public procurement project in Scotland as to make it a tourist attraction in its own right! The new crossing carries cars and lorries, leaving the original Forth Road Bridge to carry public transport, cyclists and pedestrians.

6. Sedan chair
These portable covered chairs, carried by two men, were by far the quickest and easiest way of negotiating the Old Town's narrow streets and byways. While some of the wealthy might own their own private chair, most people used public chairs in the same way that we would hail a taxi today. An example of a sedan chair 'garage' survives in Tweedale Court opposite John Knox House on the High Street.

7. The Borders Railway
By 1862 the North British Railway had completed a rail link between Edinburgh and Carlisle, running through the Scottish Borders. This double-track mainline became known as the Waverley Route, reflecting the associations of the Borders with Sir Walter Scott. Controversially, and in the face of strong local opposition, the Waverley Route was closed in 1969, leaving the Borders without any rail links. Following a vigorous public campaign, the northern part of the Waverley Route as far as Galashiels and Tweedbank (around 30 miles) re-opened on 6 September 2015. To reduce costs, the line was built as single-track, and as usage has far exceeded the

original estimates the resulting capacity constraints have resulted in frequent overcrowding and timetable delays. There are currently active proposals to re-open the rest of the Waverley Route through to Carlisle.

8. The City Bypass (A720)

When the last section opened in 1989, the City Bypass massively eased traffic congestion in the city centre. Running for 12.5 miles around the eastern edge of the built-up area, it links the main road to Glasgow (M8) with the main road south to Berwick and Newcastle (A1). Along its course it also links with the main routes south into the Borders.

9. Twelve days or more

For most of the route one would have bumped along rough tracks rather than metalled roads, progress was slow and tedious, and coaches ran once every two weeks! The early nineteenth century saw a great improvement in the quality of the roads and the introduction of regular mail coaches, so that the journey time came down to four days. However, it was the completion of the first rail link between the cities in 1846 that truly revolutionised journey times – for the first time one could reach London the same day. Modern trains make the journey in as little as 4.5 hours.

10. Because it was horse-drawn

The Edinburgh & Dalkeith Railway opened in 1831, primarily to carry coals from the Midlothian collieries into the city. The contrast between its leisurely horse-powered ways and the more dynamic steam motive power of other early lines gave rise to this charming nickname.

Sporting Edinburgh

Edinburgh people enjoy a wide range of sports, either as spectators or participants. Limber up now for a quick sprint around the city's sporting past and present.

1. Edinburgh has two main football teams. Can you name them?

2. And do you know the names of their stadiums?

3. Golf has been played in Edinburgh for hundreds of years. How many 18-hole courses are there within the city limits?

    a. 19
    b. 20
    c. 21

4. Which sport is mainly associated with Murrayfield Stadium?

5. How many times has Edinburgh hosted the Commonwealth Games?

6. During the 2014 Commonwealth Games in Glasgow, one particular sport's events were held in Edinburgh. Do you know which one?

7. Which Edinburgh sportsman has won six Olympic gold medals?

8. Which Edinburgh cricket ground is the regular home of the Scottish national cricket team?

9. Which Edinburgh-born world boxing champion was renowned for wearing bright tartan shorts in the ring?

10. Which winter sport, invented in Scotland, is played next door to Murrayfield Stadium?

Don't worry if that's tired you out – we'll be sitting down for the next round.

Answers - Round 17

1. Heart of Midlothian (Hearts) and Hibernian (Hibs)
Hearts was founded in 1874 and Hibs the following year.
The two clubs are traditional rivals, and between them have
won many trophies over their long histories, though neither
has matched the sustained success of their Glasgow counterparts, Rangers and Celtic.

2. Tynecastle (Hearts) and Easter Road (Hibs)
Hearts have played at Tynecastle since 1886. The stadium is
in the Gorgie area, to the west of the city centre. Hibs have
been based at Easter Road, to the east of the city, since 1893.

3. a. 19
The number of golf courses in the city has fluctuated slightly
over the last century, but there are currently nineteen full
18-hole courses, along with four 9-hole courses.

4. Rugby Union
Murrayfield has been the home of Scottish rugby since 1925,
and with its all-seated capacity of 67,800 is currently the
largest stadium in Scotland. A major reconstruction was
completed in 1994, when it became all-seated.

5. Twice - in 1970 and 1986
The 1970 Commonwealth Games were a great success, but
the 1986 Games were dogged by controversy as they were
boycotted by thirty-two countries over sporting links with
apartheid South Africa.

6. Diving

The Glasgow 2014 diving events were held at the Royal Commonwealth Pool, which had originally been built for the 1970 Commonwealth Games in Edinburgh.

7. Sir Chris Hoy

One of the greatest of all British Olympians, Sir Chris won medals for track cycling at every Olympics from 2000 to 2012. He retired from competitive cycling in 2013.

8. The Grange

Founded in 1832, the Grange Club is one of Edinburgh's leading sports clubs. It moved to its present location in Stockbridge in 1894, and has been the home ground of the Scottish national cricket team since 1999.

9. Ken Buchanan

As Undisputed Lightweight Champion of the World, Buchanan was a leading sporting personality in the 1970s, and reckoned by many to have been one of the greatest boxers of all time. Finally retiring in 1982, he always fought in trunks of the bright and distinctive Buchanan tartan.

10. Curling

Originating in medieval Scotland, curling was originally played outside on frozen ponds and lakes. The game involves sliding heavy granite stones towards a target area composed of four concentric circles. Curling is normally played by teams of four, and the side that wins is that which has the most stones closest to the centre of the target after all the players have thrown. It has been a sport at the Winter Olympics since 1998.

Legal Edinburgh

Edinburgh has been the centre of the Scottish legal system
– quite distinct from that in the rest of the UK – for hundreds
of years. In this round we put your knowledge on trial.

1. What is denoted by the letters 'WS'?

2. What is the name of the highest civil court in Scotland?

3. What is the name of the highest criminal court in
   Scotland?

4. What is a sheriff in Scotland?

5. What is the Scottish equivalent of a barrister?

6. What unique third verdict can juries return in criminal
   trials in Scotland?

7. What office is held by the person in charge of criminal prosecutions in Scotland?

8. What connection does Parliament Hall have with the law?

9. What is Lyon Court?

10. Which notorious eighteenth-century judge is believed to be the original of R.L. Stevenson's *Weir of Hermiston*?

Did your evidence stand up in court? If not, the next round should improve your education!

Answers - Round 18

1. Writer to the Signet

The Signet was the private seal of the Kings of Scotland, and originally Writers to the Signet were those authorised to supervise its use. They have been members of Scotland's College of Justice since it was established in 1532. Today most Writers to the Signet work as solicitors, and the Society of Writers to Her Majesty's Signet is the incorporated body to which they belong. On becoming a WS, they have to take an oath before the Keeper of the Signet, one of the Great Officers of State. The WS Society owns the magnificent A-listed Signet Library in Parliament Square, which has become one of Edinburgh's most iconic function venues.

2. The Court of Session

The Court of Session, established by James V in 1532, currently has thirty-four judges, who are known as Senators of the College of Justice. The Court is divided into the Inner House and the Outer House. Judges of the Outer House are known as Lords Ordinary, and they preside over cases of first instance, normally sitting singly. Appeals are heard in the Inner House, which is organised in two divisions. The President of the First Division is the Lord President and that of the Second the Lord Justice Clerk, his deputy. Inner House judges sit in panels of at least three, and are known as Lords of Council and Session.

3. The High Court of Justiciary

Scotland's supreme criminal court is manned by the same thirty-four judges who comprise the Court of Session in civil cases. The chief justice is the Lord Justice General (who also serves as Lord President of the Court of Session), and his deputy is the Lord Justice Clerk. The remaining judges are known as Lords Commissioners of Justiciary. Cases of first instance are heard by one judge sitting with a jury. Criminal appeals are heard by panels of two judges for appeals against sentence and three judges for appeals against conviction.

4. A judge

Perhaps disappointingly, a Scottish sheriff sports a gown and horsehair wig rather than a tin badge and a six-shooter! Originally a sheriff was a royal official, charged with keeping the peace and enforcing the king's will in a defined area of the country. Nowadays, sheriff courts are the courts in which the great majority of civil and criminal trials take place in Scotland. Serious criminal cases, such as murder, rape and armed robbery, are dealt with at the High Court (see 3 above); and similarly, the majority of high value civil cases go to the Court of Session (see 2 above). Very minor criminal matters are dealt with in Justice of the Peace Courts. Scotland is divided into six Sheriffdoms, and there are about 140 sheriffs across the country. Sheriff Court verdicts, civil or criminal, can be appealed to the higher courts.

5. An advocate

Advocates are lawyers trained to specialise in pleading in court, and are regulated by the Faculty of Advocates. Most cases in the Court of Session or the High Court are pled by advocates. They also often plead cases in the Sheriff Courts, although many of these will be pled by solicitors.

6. Not Proven

Historically, Scottish juries determined only whether the facts alleged in a trial were 'proven' or 'not proven'. In a case in 1728 the jury insisted on its right to find a defendant not guilty despite the facts being proven, and since then the three verdicts of guilty, not guilty and not proven have been open to Scottish juries. A not proven verdict is an acquittal, and the accused is free to go, as with a not guilty verdict. Many consider that the availability of this verdict is an additional safeguard for the accused, particularly as Scottish verdicts are determined by a simple majority of the fifteen-strong jury. However, its status is controversial, mainly because it is felt it carries the stigma of an implication of guilt, and there have been repeated calls for its abolition, so far without success.

7. The Lord Advocate

Her Majesty's Advocate is the chief legal officer of the Scottish Government, and in charge of the Crown Office which is the public prosecution service in Scotland. He is one of the Great Officers of State.

8. It is used by advocates to meet their clients
Parliament Hall is a glorious seventeenth-century hall with a hammer-beam roof, and was the meeting place for the old Scottish Parliament before the Union of 1707. Lined by portraits and statues of previous judges, it is part of the Court of Session complex and is open to the public.

9. The heraldic court of the Lord Lyon King of Arms
Lord Lyon is the senior herald in Scotland, charged with overseeing state ceremonial and the grant of new arms to individuals and organisations. He also sits as a judge in all cases connected with claims to arms, disputed peerages, clan chieftainships, etc. Lyon Court exercises both civil and penal jurisdiction, with the power to prosecute anyone displaying unauthorised arms. The only other surviving heraldic court in the world is in Spain.

10. Robert McQueen, Lord Braxfield (1722-1799)
A brilliant lawyer, Braxfield became a judge in 1776 and Lord Justice Clerk in 1788. Renowned for speaking 'Braid Scots', he became notorious for the severity of his judgements – particularly against political radicals – and for his often coarse humour. Many memorable quotes are assigned to him, for example, 'Let them bring me prisoners and I will find them law'; or 'Ye're a vera clever chiel, man, but ye'd be nane the waur o' a hangin'.

Education in Edinburgh

Edinburgh has been world-renowned as a centre of learning since at least the time of the eighteenth-century Enlightenment, but the story goes back several hundred years before that. Let's see if you're top of the class with these questions.

1. True or false: the University of Edinburgh is the oldest university in Scotland.

2. Which former school building dominates the view of Calton Hill from the Canongate?

3. What was the founding purpose of Donaldson's School?

4. Which school is still housed in its original seventeenth-century building?

5. Approximately what percentage of Edinburgh's school pupils is privately educated?

6. How many universities are there currently in Edinburgh?

7. Which school numbers ex-Prime Minister Tony Blair among its former pupils?

8. What is taught at New College?

9. Which profession is trained at Moray House?

10. Which school was founded particularly to improve education in classical Greek?

Time now to wander through the outskirts of Edinburgh.

Answers – Round 19

1. False

The University of Edinburgh was founded in 1582, after those
of St Andrews (1413), Glasgow (1451), and Aberdeen (1495).

2. The Royal High School

Founded in 1128, the Royal High School is one of the oldest
schools in Scotland. The magnificent neo-classical building on Calton Hill was designed by Thomas Hamilton and
completed in 1829. The school moved to a new building in
Barnton, to the west of the city, in 1968. Before the failed
devolution referendum of 1979, it had been designated as
the site for the proposed Scottish Assembly, but with the
collapse of that scheme it has been sadly under-utilised ever
since. The future use of the school is a matter of controversy.
A plan to convert it into a hotel was rejected on planning
grounds in 2015, and there are currently widely supported
proposals that it should become the new home of St Mary's
Music School.

3. A school for the deaf

Founded in 1851 through the benefaction of Sir James Donaldson, its massive Tudor-style building near Haymarket was designed by William Playfair. By the early twenty-first century the building was considered no longer suitable, and the Trust could not afford to maintain the huge premises. The site was sold, and in 2008 the school moved to new premises in Linlithgow. The old building is currently being converted into luxury apartments.

4. George Heriot's School

Founded in 1628, the school still occupies its original site in Lauriston Place, and most of its buildings date from the seventeenth century. With around 1,600 pupils, it has been co-educational since 1979, and remains one of the city's leading independent schools.

5. About 25 per cent

For various historic reasons, Edinburgh has always had a very high proportion of privately educated school pupils – in Scotland as a whole the figure is more like 4 per cent. Most of these are day schools, with the pupils returning home each evening, but there are also a number of boarding schools.

6. Four

In order of foundation these are: the University of Edinburgh; Heriot-Watt University; Edinburgh Napier University; and Queen Margaret University.

7. Fettes College

Founded in 1870 from a bequest by Sir William Fettes, a former Lord Provost of the city, Fettes is primarily a boarding school. The great gothic mass of its main building, topped by a towering spire, is a dominating sight to the north of the city, and was designed by David Bryce. Tony Blair was a pupil from 1966 to 1971. According to Ian Fleming, James Bond 007 was also educated here.

8. Divinity and theology

New College, based in the General Assembly Hall complex on the Mound, is the School of Divinity of the University of Edinburgh, and is where prospective ministers of the Church of Scotland are trained.

9. School teachers

Moray House is the School of Education of Edinburgh University, and has been involved in teacher training since 1848.

10. Edinburgh Academy

Founded in 1824, this independent day school was established because several of Edinburgh's leading citizens were dissatisfied with the level of classical education being provided by the city's existing schools. Among the founding directors was Sir Walter Scott.

ROUND 20

Districts of Edinburgh

As Edinburgh grew in the nineteenth and twentieth centuries, it absorbed many areas that were formerly thriving villages in their own right. Let's meander round some of these less central communities.

1. In which suburb is Edinburgh Zoo?

2. Which suburb of Edinburgh has given its name to an artificially refined accent?

3. What is the area of Edinburgh where Sean Connery was born and grew up?

4. Which village, secluded along the banks of the Water of Leith yet only a few minutes' walk from Princes Street, was one of Edinburgh's earliest industrial areas?

5. Which Edinburgh village claims to have the oldest pub in Scotland?

6. Which district acquired its name from the French courtiers of Mary Queen of Scots?

7. Which Edinburgh suburb is named after a port in modern Israel?

8. What picturesque village on the outskirts of Edinburgh boasts thatched cottages and a close connection with Robert Louis Stevenson?

9. Which famous Edinburgh artist was born in Stockbridge, and was largely responsible for the district's development?

10. Which area of Edinburgh derives its name from a Dominican convent that formerly stood there?

Did you enjoy your stroll? You'll need to be relaxed before tackling the next round!

Answers – Round 20

1. Corstorphine
Opened in 1913 by the Royal Zoological Society of Scotland, the zoo is one of Edinburgh's leading attractions, with about 600,000 visitors a year. From its earliest days it has been renowned for its penguins, and the daily Penguin Parade is not to be missed. In 2011 the zoo acquired two Giant Pandas, Yang Guang and Tian Tian, from China, which have proved a huge draw for visitors.

2. Morningside
This prosperous suburb on the Southside has become synonymous with the over-articulated speech of some middle-class Scots. One of its distinguishing characteristics is a tendency to elongate vowel sounds. Thus 'that' emerges as 'thet' or 'time' as 'taime'. The old joke is that in Morningside 'sex' is what they deliver the coal in!

3. Fountainbridge
Sean Connery was born in this working-class area a short distance west of the city centre in 1930.

4. Dean Village
Almost hidden from view in the deep gorge of the Water of Leith, Dean Village is now an oasis of semi-rural tranquillity just a few minutes' walk from the bustle of Princes Street. For hundreds of years it was the city's centre of grain milling, with up to eleven mills utilising the river's fast-flowing currents.

5. Duddingston

The Sheep Heid Inn claims to have been established on the same site in 1360, though, of course, the original building has long been replaced. It remains, however, a pub of great character and still has an old-fashioned skittles alley dating from Victorian times. The name may derive from two local delicacies of the past – sheep heid broth and singed sheep heid. The inn is still renowned for serving good food, although these two items no longer figure on the menu! In July 2016 patrons were astonished when Her Majesty the Queen popped in for dinner on her way back to Holyrood Palace from the Musselburgh races.

6. Little France

About 4 miles south of the city centre, Little France nestles under the medieval bulk of Craigmillar Castle. When Mary Queen of Scots returned to Scotland from France she often liked to stay at Craigmillar, away from the Old Town's congestion and smells. The name derives from her French courtiers who lived in this adjacent area. Since 2003 Little France has been the site of one of the city's principal hospitals, the Royal Infirmary of Edinburgh, which relocated here from its city centre location on Lauriston Place.

7. Joppa

This suburb, lying between Portobello and Musselburgh on the Firth of Forth, has been known as Joppa since the late eighteenth century. The name derives from the Latin name of Jaffa, the ancient Biblical port city now in modern Israel. Quite why it was felt an appropriate name for a village in Scotland remains a mystery!

8. Swanston

Nestling at the foot of the Pentland Hills on the south side of the City Bypass, this improbably picturesque little village, with its whitewashed thatched cottages, is where Robert Louis Stevenson spent several summers after his father took a lease on a house there. It is the setting for his unfinished novel *St. Ives*.

9. Sir Henry Raeburn (1756-1823)

Raeburn was a truly inspired portrait painter, and painted many of the leading lights of the Edinburgh Enlightenment. When looking at one of his portraits, the subject seems to come to life, and the character, warts and all, shines through. Perhaps his most famous painting is *The Rev Robert Walker Skating on Duddingston Loch*, familiarly known as 'The Skating Minister'. His New Town studio in York Place is, fittingly, almost opposite the Scottish National Portrait Gallery where many of his works are displayed.

10. Sciennes

This suburb, lying just south of the Meadows, takes its name from the former Convent of Our Lady of Sienna (*Sienne* in French). It is pronounced 'Sheens'.

ROUND 21

Political Edinburgh

Edinburgh has been Scotland's capital since the fifteenth century, so politics has always been at the heart of the city's life. Some of these waters may be murky, but they are central to the city's identity.

1. Which party is currently governing Scotland?

2. And what is currently the largest opposition party in the Scottish Parliament?

3. A referendum was held in Scotland in September 2014. Do you know what it was about?

4. How many Members of the Scottish Parliament (MSPs) are there in total?

5. What is the official title of the speaker of the Scottish Parliament?

6. What was the Scottish Government called from 1999 until 2007?

7. Where did the devolved Scottish Parliament meet from 1999 until its new building was completed in 2004?

8. Which building on Calton Hill, completed in 1939, is the headquarters of the Scottish Government?

9. In the past, what was a Scottish representative peer?

10. What controversial law reform did the Scottish Government drop in 2015 following intense opposition from the legal profession?

After that, you may need the sweet fragrance of a pot pourri!

Answers - Round 21

1. The Scottish National Party (SNP)

The SNP's primary purpose is to secure Scottish independence. After many years in the political wilderness, it became the largest party in the Scottish Parliament in the 2007 Scottish Election, and has formed the Scottish Government since then. At the 2011 election, the SNP achieved an overall majority in the Parliament, but lost this at the 2016 election, although it remains in office as the largest party. At the time of writing, the leader of the SNP, and First Minister of Scotland, is Nicola Sturgeon.

2. The Scottish Conservative & Unionist Party (Scottish Tories)

The biggest shock of the 2016 Scottish election was the emergence of the Conservatives as the second largest party in the Scottish Parliament and the official opposition to the SNP government. For thirty years or more the Tories had been the pariahs of Scottish politics, largely because of the unpopularity in Scotland of the Thatcher administration in the 1980s. Under a dynamic new young leader, Ruth Davidson, the party managed at least partly to shake off that legacy, and overtook the Labour Party, which had dominated Scottish politics for decades.

3. Scottish independence

Using the overall majority it had in the 2011 Scottish Parliament, the SNP passed legislation calling a referendum on Scottish independence, which was held on 18 September 2014. The question put to the electorate was: 'Should Scotland be an independent country?' to which one could vote Yes or No. Despite an imaginative and enthusiastic Yes campaign and a rather lacklustre No campaign, the eventual outcome was a fairly decisive 55 per cent No to 45 per cent Yes vote. There is pressure from SNP activists for a further referendum, although opinion polling suggests little movement in popular opinion since 2014.

4. 129

This total comprises seventy-three constituency members, elected on a first past the post basis, and a further fifty-six members elected on a regional list basis, using a form of proportional representation.

5. Presiding Officer

At the time of writing the Presiding Officer is Ken Macintosh MSP.

6. The Scottish Executive

This was the official title given to the devolved administration in 1999 by the relevant Westminster legislation. In addition, for the first eight years after devolution the Scottish administration was formed by a coalition between the Labour and Liberal Democrat Parties, who felt that the term 'Government' smacked too much of independence. On gaining office in 2007 the SNP immediately rebranded the Executive as the Scottish Government. Further Westminster legislation in 2012 formalised this change of name.

7. The General Assembly Hall on the Mound

While the new Parliament Building was under construction (see Round 12, question 1), the Parliament held its debates in the General Assembly Hall of the Church of Scotland. In two years (1999 and 2001) this meant the Kirk had to find alternative venues for its General Assembly.

8. St Andrew's House

Built on the site of the old Calton Gaol, St Andrew's House was originally the Edinburgh base of the Scottish Office, including the offices of the Secretary of State for Scotland. Following devolution, it is now the headquarters of the Scottish Government and includes the offices of the First Minister and several other Scottish ministers. Around 1,400 civil servants work there.

9. One of sixteen Scottish peers elected to sit in the House of Lords

Following the Union of the Parliaments in 1707, Scottish peers, unlike their English counterparts, did not enjoy an automatic right to sit in the House of Lords. Instead Scottish peers elected sixteen of their number to sit in the Lords. They sat for a single term and after each Parliament was dissolved there was a fresh election of Scottish peers. (Many Scottish peers also acquired British peerages, which did carry an automatic right to sit in the Lords). This system ended in 1963, when all Scottish peers acquired the right to membership of the Lords. Curiously, a variant on this system has reappeared following reform of the House of Lords in 1999. Hereditary peers no longer sit as of right in the Lords, but instead elect ninety-two of their number to serve in the Second Chamber.

10. The proposal to abolish corroboration

It is a cornerstone of Scots criminal law that at least two independent sources of evidence for material facts are required before an accused can be convicted of a crime. This means, for example, that a confession alone is insufficient to secure conviction as it is uncorroborated, and also explains why Scottish police officers always patrol in pairs. Corroboration often takes the form of more than one witness, but forensic or circumstantial evidence can also be used in corroboration. Because of concern at low conviction rates in cases of rape and domestic abuse the Scottish Government proposed abolishing corroboration, but backed down in 2015 in the face of intense opposition from the legal profession and civil liberties campaigners.

ROUND 22

Edinburgh Pot Pourri

Well, we've covered a fair bit of ground! Let's finish with a general miscellaneous round, catching some aspects we've missed under the specific themes so far.

1. What is Edinburgh's population to the nearest 50,000?

2. What is Edinburgh's best-known nickname?

3. Approximately how many listed buildings are there in Edinburgh?

    a. 200
    b. 1,800
    c. 4,500

4. What popular confection bears the city's name?

5. Who masterminded George IV's visit to Edinburgh in 1822?

6. What department store is known as 'Edinburgh's Harrods'?

7. Which canal used to terminate at Port Hopetoun near Lothian Road?

8. John Napier, the inventor of logarithms, lived in which castle?

   a. Craigmillar
   b. Lauriston
   c. Merchiston

9. Until it closed in 1995, what sport would you go to see at Powderhall Stadium?

10. What were the Wells o' Wearie used for?

Well, that's it – our tour of Edinburgh is over for now. But we've barely scratched the surface of this beautiful, endlessly fascinating city. It's been a real pleasure showing you round, but I hope you'll be back soon, to explore it more fully in the company of one of Scotland's expert Blue Badge guides!

Answers – Round 22

1. 500,000

The city's population in the 2011 census was 486,120. The estimated population at the time of writing is just over 495,000.

2. Auld Reekie

This name means 'Old Smoky', but may also have some reference to the stench arising from the former sanitary arrangements in the Old Town (see Round 1, question 7)! A striking feature of Edinburgh, on which visitors frequently comment, is the huge number of chimney pots on the roofline. Over the last fifty years clean air legislation has stopped the use of coal fires in the city, but until then each of these chimneys would have been belching black smoke, and many old photographs of Edinburgh show a smoky pall hovering over the city centre. Thankfully, both the smoke and the smell are now things of the past!

3. c. 4,500

Around 900 of these are Category A listed, which represents almost 25 per cent of the total Category A listings in the whole of Scotland. (Listed buildings have been placed on a statutory register of buildings of architectural or historic interest. They may not be demolished or altered without special permission from the relevant planning authorities.)

4. Edinburgh rock

This sweet delight has been popular since Victorian times. Unlike ordinary rock, it has a soft, crumbly texture.

5. Sir Walter Scott

In August 1822 King George IV made the first visit to Scotland by a reigning monarch since Charles II in 1651. Scott seized the opportunity to stage a splendid pageant celebrating Scotland's ancient past – in particular its Highland heritage. The result was a riot of tartan, plaids and bagpipes, with even the portly King being persuaded to wear Highland dress. Although the 'King's Jaunt' attracted some ridicule south of the Border, it was accounted a great success in Scotland. It helped to establish the iconic connection between Scotland and tartan that still largely forms the world's impression of this country.

6. Jenners

Founded in 1838, this Princes Street landmark remained an independent family owned concern until 2005, when it was acquired by House of Fraser.

7. The Union Canal

This canal was opened in 1822 to connect Edinburgh with the Forth and Clyde Canal near Falkirk, and so through to Glasgow and the River Clyde. Initially a huge commercial success, it faded rapidly after the opening of the Edinburgh & Glasgow Railway in 1842. It was officially closed in 1965, but with the growth of recreational boating was reopened in 2001, and in 2002 was once more joined to the Forth and Clyde Canal with the completion of the Falkirk Wheel, a giant rotating boat lift. The original eastern terminus at Port Hopetoun was closed as long ago as 1921, and the canal now terminates at Lochrin Basin off Fountainbridge.

8. c. Merchiston

John Napier (1550-1617) was a brilliant mathematician and astronomer. He also happened to be a Scottish Laird who was born and died in the family seat of Merchiston Castle. Edinburgh Napier University (named after the great man) has the castle at the centre of its Merchiston campus.

9. Greyhound racing

Opened in 1927, the track closed in 1995 when it was sold and developed for housing.

10. A place for washing clothes

The Wells o' Wearie, in Holyrood Park near Duddingston Loch, were used by the local washerwomen, who laid out their clothes to dry and bleach nearby. This practice stopped in the 1840s, by which time it had become a popular, romantic destination for a recreational stroll. Still standing nearby is Wells o' Wearie Cottage, originally built in the 1850s for the shepherd in charge of the sheep that used to graze in Holyrood Park until the 1970s. The Wells are celebrated in a popular Scots song:

> Come, let us spend a simmer day
> Beside the Wells o' Wearie!

ALSO IN THIS SERIES

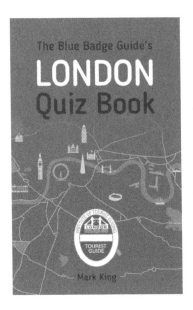

The Blue Badge Guide's London Quiz Book
978 0 7509 6823 2

Drawing on extensive knowledge and celebrating London's diverse riches, this quiz book invites you to come on a wide-ranging exploration of the megacity the author calls 'The Big Onion'. Peel away its many layers in the company of one of London's top Blue Badge tourist guides. These 22 rounds will inspire you, your family, colleagues and friends to leap from page to pavement in the entertaining company of a local expert. Have fun!